Taste of Home

ALL-NEW
Christmas Cookies

THIS BOOK IS GIVEN TO:

WITH HEARTWARMING WISHES FROM:

TASTE OF HOME BOOKS • RDA ENTHUSIAST BRANDS, LLC • MILWAUKEE, WI

Visit us at **tasteofhome.com** for other Taste of Home books and products.

International Standard Book Number: 978-1-62145-986-6

Chief Content Officer, Home & Garden: Jeanne Sidner
Content Director: Mark Hagen
Creative Director: Raeann Thompson
Senior Editors: Christine Rukavena, Julie Schnittka
Editor: Hazel Wheaton
Assistant Editor: Sammi DiVito
Senior Art Director: Courtney Lovetere
Art Director: Maggie Conners
Designer: Sierra Schuler
Deputy Editor, Copy Desk: Dulcie Shoener

Cover Photography
Photographer: Jim Wieland
Set Stylist: Melissa Franco
Food Stylist: Lauren Knoelke

Pictured on front cover:
Santa Star Cookies, p. 24; Gingerbread Snowflakes, p. 27;
Yeti Cookies, p. 26; Best-Ever Cutout Cookies, p. 32;
Eggnog Cookies, p. 13; JoJo's Ginger Cookies, p. 21

Pictured on back cover:
Reindeer Brownies, p. 125;
Holiday Sugar Cookies, p. 156;
Peppermint Candy Sandwich Cookies, p. 179;
Cherry Cranberry Pinwheels, p. 175;
Glazed Cherry Bonbon Cookies, p. 94

Pictured on spine:
Roly-Poly Santas, p. 70

Printed in China
1 3 5 7 9 10 8 6 4 2

TABLE OF CONTENTS

More ways to connect with us:

SHOPTASTEOFHOME.COM

Christmastime Is Cookie Time!

There are some things you can count on appearing every Christmas season: Holiday songs playing in every store. A decked-out tree in the town center. Santa Claus taking photos with kids and hearing their whispered Christmas wishes. The neighbor's house (or your own!) brightly lit and lavishly decorated. And, of course, cookies. Lots and lots and *lots* of cookies.

Plates of cookies at the office. Tins filled with cookies as thank-you gifts for teachers and neighbors. Elaborate trays of cookies set out for house guests. Boxes of cookies carefully packed up and sent to loved ones far away.

With this new collection, you can make your cookies the centerpiece of every celebration. From over 100 recipes, you can select just what the occasion calls for. Adorable Penguin Cutouts (p. 16) for a school event,

elegant Mocha Meringue Sandwich Cookies (p. 121) as a light post-feast treat, Chocolate Rum Balls (p. 200) for a grown-up party, gorgeous Bite-Sized Cinnamon Roll Cookies (p. 168) to be tucked into a care package.

This new collection also includes valuable advice on how to create your own stunning cookie tray (opposite page), how to host a cookie exchange party (p. 9), how to ship cookies so they arrive fresh and unbroken (p. 7), and creative ideas for gift packaging (p. 6)—sound advice you'll use every year!

All the recipes are the family favorites of talented home bakers like you, and have been rigorously tested so you know they'll work. Add in dozens of tips from the experts in the *Taste of Home* Test Kitchen, and you're all set to make your cookies the ones everyone will rave about this Christmas!

The Perfect Cookie Plate

Your cookies may be miniature works of art—but arranging them on a platter can be an art of its own. A thoughtful plate design not only shows off the cookies to their best advantage, but it also keeps them tasting their best and makes it easier for your guests to not just admire, but enjoy!

1. Choose a Serving Tray

Whether you're arranging cookies in a box or on a tray or platter, its size is the first consideration. Too large, and the cookies will appear underwhelming; too small, and you'll have an unwieldy mess. If you have space, use several trays or plates—it's easier for guests to help themselves if they're not crowding around a single dish. Simple colors will make your cookies the star of the show.

2. Include a Variety of Cookies

Variety is key to creating a tempting cookie tray—but you don't need to make every cookie in the book or include every cookie you've made on the tray. Stick with some five to seven varieties to keep things interesting yet not overwhelming. Include a few nostalgic, surefire classics as well as some adventurous new recipes.

3. Keep Textures and Flavors Together

To keep cookies at their best, organize similar types together. Strongly flavored cookies, such as mint or molasses cookies, can transfer their flavor to milder sugar cookies. Soft cookies can transfer moisture to crisper cookies. Add Christmas candies between different types of cookies to make a decorative (and tasty) border.

4. Think Geometrically

Round cookies work well arranged in concentric circles. Put a single cookie in the center of the tray, then arrange the rest of the cookies in circles around the central cookie. Square or rectangular cookies are ideal for horizontal or vertical designs. Layer one cookie slightly on top of the next to create texture in your display.

5. Consider Food Allergies

If you know that some of your guests have food allergies, prepare and organize separate platters with allergen-friendly cookies. Add labels to identify gluten-free, nut-free, dairy-free or other allergen-free treats. Be ready to answer any questions about what's in your cookies—and to be extra helpful, have a list of ingredients on hand for each cookie.

Mexican Tea Cookies

These cookies are a holiday favorite in our family. I updated the
recipe by frosting them with a buttercream made with dulce de leche.
They are a tender, crumbly cookie that everyone enjoys.
—*David Ross, Spokane Valley, WA*

PREP: 45 MIN. + CHILLING • **BAKE:** 10 MIN./BATCH + COOLING • **MAKES:** 3 DOZEN

1 cup butter, softened
½ cup confectioners'
sugar
½ cup sugar
1 large egg, room
temperature
1 tsp. vanilla extract
3¼ cups all-purpose flour
¾ cup finely chopped
pecans
1 tsp. baking powder
¼ tsp. salt
¼ tsp. ground cinnamon

BUTTERCREAM
½ cup butter, softened
1 Tbsp. heavy whipping
cream
1 tsp. vanilla extract
2 cups confectioners'
sugar
½ cup dulce de leche
2 Tbsp. ground pecans

1. In a large bowl, cream butter and sugars until light
and fluffy, 5-7 minutes. Beat in egg and vanilla. In another
bowl, whisk the flour, pecans, baking powder, salt and
cinnamon; gradually beat into creamed mixture. Dough
will be soft. Form dough into a disk; cover and refrigerate
1 hour or until chilled.

2. Preheat oven to 350°. On a floured surface, roll the
dough to ¼-in. thickness. Cut with a floured 2-in. round
cookie cutter; reroll dough scraps as needed. Place 2 in.
apart on parchment-lined baking sheets.

3. Bake until edges begin to lightly brown, 10-12 minutes.
Remove from pans to wire racks to cool completely.

4. For buttercream, in a large bowl, beat butter, cream
and vanilla until creamy. Beat in confectioners' sugar
alternately with dulce de leche until smooth. Sprinkle
the cookies with additional confectioners' sugar. Pipe
buttercream onto cookies; sprinkle with pecans. Store,
covered, in refrigerator.

NOTE: This recipe was tested with Nestle La Lechera dulce
de leche; look for it in the international foods section. If
using Eagle Brand dulce de leche (caramel flavored sauce),
thicken according to package directions before using.

1 COOKIE: 188 cal., 10g fat (5g sat. fat), 27mg chol., 101mg
sod., 23g carb. (13g sugars, 1g fiber), 2g pro.

Eggnog Cookies

This cookie's flavor fits right into the holiday spirit—pick your favorite cookie cutter shapes to make them even more festive!
—*Myra Innes, Auburn, KS*

PREP: 25 MIN. + CHILLING • **BAKE:** 10 MIN./BATCH + COOLING • **MAKES:** ABOUT 7 DOZEN

1 **cup butter, softened**
2 **cups sugar**
1 **cup eggnog**
1 **tsp. baking soda**
½ **tsp. ground nutmeg**
5½ **cups all-purpose flour**
1 **large egg white,**
  lightly beaten
  Colored sugar
  Vanilla frosting,
  optional

1. In a large bowl, cream the butter and sugar until light and fluffy, 5-7 minutes. Beat in the eggnog, baking soda and nutmeg. Gradually add flour and mix well. Cover and chill 1 hour.

2. Preheat oven to 350°. On a lightly floured surface, roll out half the dough to ⅛-in. thickness. Using floured 3½-in. cookie cutters, cut into desired shapes; place on ungreased baking sheets. Repeat with remaining dough. Brush with egg white; sprinkle with colored sugar.

3. Bake until edges are lightly browned, 6-8 minutes. Remove from pans to wire racks to cool completely. If desired, decorate with frosting.

NOTE: This recipe was tested with commercially prepared eggnog.

1 COOKIE: 71 cal., 2g fat (1g sat. fat), 8mg chol., 35mg sod., 11g carb. (5g sugars, 0 fiber), 1g pro.

READER REVIEW
"This is a 5-star hit with my family. I love the flavor, and the dough rolled out nicely. I will be adding this to my Christmas cookie list every year."
—BILLIEPOCK, TASTEOFHOME.COM

Peppermint Schnapps Hot Cocoa Snowflakes

Mint and chocolate are perfect partners in these cutout cookies!
Replace the frosting with a chocolate glaze for even more indulgence.
—James Schend, Pleasant Prairie, WI

PREP: 1 HOUR • BAKE: 10 MIN./BATCH + COOLING • MAKES: ABOUT 4 DOZEN

1 cup butter, softened
1½ cups sugar
2 large eggs, room temperature
1 tsp. vanilla extract
1 tsp. instant espresso powder
3 cups all-purpose flour
⅔ cup baking cocoa
½ tsp. baking powder
¼ tsp. salt

ICING
1 pkg. (1 lb.) confectioners' sugar
6 Tbsp. shortening
¼ cup peppermint schnapps
2 to 3 Tbsp. water
Food coloring, optional

1. In a large bowl, cream butter and sugar until light and fluffy, 5-7 minutes. Beat in eggs, vanilla and espresso powder. In another bowl, whisk flour, cocoa, baking powder and salt; gradually beat into creamed mixture. Divide dough in half.

2. Preheat oven to 350°. Roll each portion of dough to ¼-in. thickness between 2 sheets of waxed paper. Cut with floured 3-in. snowflake cookie cutters. Place 1 in. apart on ungreased baking sheets.

3. Bake 10-12 minutes or until set. Remove from pans to wire racks to cool completely.

4. For icing, in a large bowl, beat confectioners' sugar, shortening, schnapps and enough water to reach a spreading consistency. If desired, add 4 drops food coloring to the inside of a pastry bag fitted with a small star tip. Decorate cookies as desired. Let stand at room temperature until frosting is dry and firm.

FREEZE OPTION: Freeze cookies, layered between waxed paper, in freezer containers. To use, thaw before serving.

1 COOKIE: 147 cal., 6g fat (3g sat. fat), 18mg chol., 51mg sod., 22g carb. (16g sugars, 0 fiber), 1g pro.

Penguin Cutouts

Your children can help cut out and decorate these cute cookies.
It's a memory-making way to get them involved in the kitchen!
—Taste of Home *Test Kitchen*

PREP: 1½ HOURS + CHILLING • **BAKE:** 10 MIN./BATCH + COOLING • **MAKES:** 3 DOZEN

½ cup butter-flavored shortening
1 cup sugar
1 large egg, room temperature
1½ tsp. vanilla extract
½ cup sour cream
2¾ cups all-purpose flour
½ tsp. baking soda
½ tsp. salt

FROSTING
3¾ cups confectioners' sugar
⅓ cup water
4 tsp. meringue powder
Black, orange, red and green paste food coloring
Edible ink pen, optional

1. In a large bowl, cream the shortening and sugar until light and fluffy, 5-7 minutes. Beat in the egg and vanilla. Stir in sour cream. Combine flour, baking soda and salt; gradually add to creamed mixture and mix well. Divide dough into 3 balls; cover and refrigerate 3 hours or until easy to handle.

2. Preheat oven to 375°. Remove 1 portion of dough from the refrigerator at a time. On a lightly floured surface, roll out dough to ⅛-in. thickness. Cut with a floured 4-in. penguin cookie cutter. Place 1 in. apart on ungreased baking sheets.

3. Bake 6-8 minutes or until edges are lightly browned. Remove to wire racks to cool.

4. For frosting, in a small bowl, combine confectioners' sugar, water and meringue powder; beat on low speed just until combined. Beat on high 4 minutes or until soft peaks form. Set aside half the frosting to remain white.

5. Tint half the remaining frosting black. Divide the rest into thirds; tint 1 orange, 1 red and 1 green. Store frostings in airtight containers when not in use. Beat again on high speed to restore texture as needed between uses.

6. Working quickly with the black frosting, pipe outlines of the penguins' bodies; fill in with thinned black frosting. Let dry at room temperature for several hours or until firm. Fill in centers of penguins with thinned white frosting; let dry until firm.

7. Add eyes with the black and white frostings or edible-ink pen. Add orange beaks and feet and red and green scarves. Let stand until set. Add white and contrasting-colored polka dots on the scarves. Let stand until set. Store in an airtight container.

1 COOKIE: 139 cal., 4g fat (1g sat. fat), 6mg chol., 56mg sod., 26g carb. (18g sugars, 0 fiber), 1g pro.

Brown Sugar Cutout Cookies

Our neighbor made these for me when I was little, and now I make
them for my kids and grandkids and for the children at school.
Serve them with milk for the kids and tea for the grown-ups.
—*Nancy Lynch, Somerset, PA*

PREP: 55 MIN. + CHILLING • **BAKE:** 10 MIN./BATCH + COOLING • **MAKES:** 7½ DOZEN

1 cup butter, softened
2 cups packed dark
  brown sugar
3 large eggs, room
  temperature
6 Tbsp. cold water
3 Tbsp. canola oil
1 tsp. vanilla extract
6 cups all-purpose flour
1 tsp. cream of tartar
1 tsp. baking soda
½ tsp. salt

ICING
1 cup butter, softened
4 tsp. meringue powder
3 tsp. cream of tartar
½ tsp. salt
4 cups confectioners'
  sugar
4 to 6 Tbsp. water
  Assorted sprinkles,
  optional

1. In a large bowl, cream butter and brown sugar until light and fluffy, 5-7 minutes. Beat in eggs, water, oil and vanilla. In another bowl, whisk flour, cream of tartar, baking soda and salt; gradually beat into creamed mixture.

2. Divide the dough into 4 portions. Shape each into a disk; wrap. Refrigerate 2 hours or until firm enough to roll.

3. Preheat oven to 350°. On a lightly floured surface, roll each portion of dough to ⅛-in. thickness. Cut with a floured 2¼-in. fluted square cookie cutter. Place 1 in. apart on greased baking sheets.

4. Bake 7-9 minutes or until bottoms are light brown. Remove from pans to wire racks to cool completely.

5. For the icing, in a small bowl, beat butter, meringue powder, cream of tartar and salt until blended. Beat in confectioners' sugar alternately with enough water to reach a spreading consistency. Spread over cookies. If desired, top with sprinkles. Let stand until set.

1 COOKIE: 113 cal., 5g fat (3g sat. fat), 17mg chol., 78mg sod., 17g carb. (10g sugars, 0 fiber), 1g pro.

Cranberry Shortbread Stars

My family loves shortbread and I love cranberries, so I decided to put the two together. The star shape is a festive addition to my holiday cookie tray.
—*Sonya Labbe, West Hollywood, CA*

PREP: 20 MIN. + CHILLING • **BAKE:** 15 MIN./BATCH • **MAKES:** ABOUT 3 DOZEN

1 **cup butter, softened**
¾ **cup confectioners' sugar**
½ **tsp. salt**
1 **tsp. vanilla extract**
2 **cups all-purpose flour**
½ **cup finely chopped dried cranberries**

1. In a large bowl, beat butter, confectioners' sugar and salt until blended. Beat in vanilla. Gradually beat in flour. Stir in cranberries.

2. Shape the dough into a disk. Cover and refrigerate for 30 minutes or until firm enough to roll.

3. Preheat the oven to 325°. On a lightly floured surface, roll dough to ¼-in. thickness. Cut with a floured 2-in. star-shaped cookie cutter. Place 1 in. apart on greased baking sheets.

4. Bake 12-15 minutes or until edges are golden brown. Remove from pans to wire racks to cool.

1 COOKIE: 87 cal., 5g fat (3g sat. fat), 14mg chol., 74mg sod., 10g carb. (4g sugars, 0 fiber), 1g pro.

CHILL OUT!
It's important to chill the dough before rolling it out because it will make the dough easier to work with and the dough won't stick to the roller or cutter. You may also want to chill the cutout cookies before baking them. Doing so will give the finished cookies a cleaner edge, whereas room-temperature dough will spread more as soon as it hits the heat.

JoJo's Ginger Cookies

We created gingery cutout cookies to go with a book made especially for my niece's third-grade class. The crispy golden brown cookies stole the show.
—*Jenet Cattar, Neptune Beach, FL*

PREP: 40 MIN. + FREEZING • BAKE: 10 MIN./BATCH • MAKES: ABOUT 1½ DOZEN

½ cup shortening
½ cup packed brown
  sugar
½ cup molasses
¼ cup water
3 cups all-purpose flour
1 tsp. ground ginger
½ tsp. ground nutmeg
⅛ tsp. ground allspice
½ tsp. baking soda
½ tsp. salt
  **Vanilla frosting and
  nonpareils, optional**

1. In a large bowl, cream shortening and brown sugar until light and fluffy, 5-7 minutes. Beat in molasses and water. In another bowl, whisk flour, spices, baking soda and salt; gradually beat into creamed mixture.

2. Divide dough in half. Shape each into a disk; place in a covered freezer container, separated by waxed paper. Freeze until firm enough to roll, about 1 hour.

3. Preheat oven to 375°. On a floured surface, roll each portion of dough to ¼-in. thickness. Cut with a floured 5-in. cookie cutter. Carefully place 1 in. apart on ungreased baking sheets. Bake until set, 7-9 minutes. Cool on pans 5 minutes. Remove to wire racks to cool. If desired, pipe with vanilla frosting and decorate with nonpareils.

FREEZE OPTION: Transfer wrapped disks to a covered freezer container, separated by waxed paper; freeze. To use, thaw dough in refrigerator until soft enough to roll. Prepare and bake as directed.

1 COOKIE: 157 cal., 5g fat (1g sat. fat), 0 chol., 95mg sod., 26g carb. (11g sugars, 1g fiber), 2g pro.

A LESSON IN MOLASSES
Molasses comes in light and dark varieties. Light molasses is the most popular type because it has the highest sugar content and a mild flavor. Dark molasses is thick with a deep, rich flavor and isn't as sweet. Either can be used in baking.

Egg Yolk Cookies

These cookies taste just like the ones my grandma used to make.
They truly melt in your mouth, thanks to the hard-boiled egg yolks.
—*Kathy Gagliardi, Holmdel, NJ*

PREP: 20 MIN. + CHILLING • **BAKE:** 15 MIN./BATCH + COOLING • **MAKES:** 6 DOZEN

4 hard-boiled large egg yolks
1 cup unsalted butter, softened
½ cup sugar
1 Tbsp. vanilla extract
2½ cups all-purpose flour
Dash salt
1 raw large egg yolk, lightly beaten

1. Press the hard-boiled egg yolks through a fine-mesh strainer into a bowl. In a large bowl, cream butter and sugar until light and fluffy, 5-7 minutes. Beat in strained egg yolks and vanilla. In another bowl, whisk flour and salt; gradually beat into creamed mixture. Divide dough in half. Shape each into a disk; wrap. Refrigerate 30 minutes or until firm enough to roll.

2. Preheat oven to 350°. On a lightly floured surface, roll each portion of dough to ¼-in. thickness. Cut with a floured 2-in. fluted cookie cutter. Place 1 in. apart on parchment-lined baking sheets. Brush with the beaten egg yolk.

3. Bake until lightly browned, 12-14 minutes. Remove from pans to wire racks to cool.

1 COOKIE: 46 cal., 3g fat (2g sat. fat), 19mg chol., 3mg sod., 5g carb. (1g sugars, 0 fiber), 1g pro.

> **HARD-BOILED EGG HOW-TO**
> To make hard-boiled eggs, place the eggs in a single layer in a saucepan and add enough water to cover the eggs by 1 in. Cover and quickly bring to a boil over high heat. Remove the pan from the heat and let stand for 15 minutes. Rinse the eggs in cold water, then place in an ice water bath until completely cooled.

Gingerbread Snowflakes

Our tradition is to make snowflake cookies to eat in the car
on our way to fetch a Christmas tree. These are a favorite.
—*Shelly Rynearson, Oconomowoc, WI*

PREP: 30 MIN. + CHILLING • **BAKE:** 10 MIN./BATCH + COOLING • **MAKES:** 5 DOZEN

1 **cup butter, softened**
1 **cup sugar**
1 **cup molasses**
¼ **cup water**
5 **cups all-purpose flour**
2½ **tsp. ground ginger**
1½ **tsp. baking soda**
1½ **tsp. ground cinnamon**
½ **tsp. ground allspice**
¼ **tsp. salt**

FROSTING
3¾ **cups confectioners'**
sugar
¼ **cup water**
1½ **tsp. light corn syrup**
½ **tsp. vanilla extract**

1. In a large bowl, cream butter and sugar until light and fluffy, 5-7 minutes. Beat in molasses and water. Combine the flour, ginger, baking soda, cinnamon, allspice and salt; gradually add to creamed mixture and mix well. Cover and refrigerate for 1 hour or until easy to handle.

2. On a lightly floured surface, roll out to ¼-in. thickness. Cut with 2½-in. cookie cutters dipped in flour. Place 2 in. apart on ungreased baking sheets.

3. Bake at 350° until the edges are firm, 10-12 minutes. Remove to wire racks to cool.

4. In a small bowl, combine the frosting ingredients; beat until smooth. Transfer to a pastry bag fitted with a tip; pipe frosting onto cookies in desired designs.

1 COOKIE: 124 cal., 3g fat (2g sat. fat), 8mg chol., 68mg sod., 23g carb. (15g sugars, 0 fiber), 1g pro.

READER REVIEW
"These turned out great! They were not too hard and not too soft and had just the right amount of spice for my family."
—SEATTLEFRETTCHEN, TASTEOFHOME.COM

Christmas Tree Cookies

Delight family and friends with these holly jolly evergreens.
Iced with creamy frosting and dusted with sparkly colored sugars,
the 3D cookie trees are as delicious as they are beautiful.
—Taste of Home *Test Kitchen*

PREP: 1½ HOURS • **BAKE:** 10 MIN./BATCH + COOLING
MAKES: 18-36 COOKIE TREES, DEPENDING ON FULLNESS

1   **cup butter, softened**
1¼ **cups sugar**
2   **large eggs, room temperature**
2   **tsp. vanilla extract**
3½ **cups all-purpose flour**
2   **tsp. baking powder**
    Green gel or paste food coloring

ROYAL ICING
4½ **cups confectioners' sugar**
½   **cup warm water**
3   **Tbsp. meringue powder**
1   **tsp. vanilla extract**
½   **tsp. cream of tartar**
    Green gel or paste food coloring
    Assorted decorating sprinkles and white edible glitter

1. In a large bowl, cream butter and sugar until light and fluffy, 5-7 minutes. Add eggs, 1 at a time, beating well after each addition. Beat in vanilla. Combine flour and baking powder; gradually add to creamed mixture and mix well.

2. Divide the dough in half. Tint half of the dough green; knead well to distribute color evenly. Leave remaining dough white. Cover and refrigerate for 1 hour or until easy to handle.

3. Preheat oven to 350°. On a lightly floured surface, roll out each portion of dough to ⅛-in. thickness. Use tree-shaped cookie cutters with identical shapes, measuring 2½ in., 3 in., 4 in. and 4½ in. Cut out an even number of cookies with each size cookie cutter.

4. Place 1 in. apart on ungreased baking sheets. Bake until golden brown, 8-10 minutes. Immediately cut half of each size tree cookies in half from top to bottom. If tree cookie cutters have trunks, trim trunks off trees, creating a flat base. Remove to wire racks to cool.

5. For frosting, in a large bowl, combine confectioners' sugar, water, meringue powder, vanilla and cream of tartar. Beat on high speed for 8-10 minutes or until stiff peaks form. Divide frosting in half. Tint half of the frosting green; leave remaining frosting white. Cover frosting with damp paper towels between uses.

TO GLAZE TREES: In a small bowl, thin 1 cup green frosting with 2-3 Tbsp. water until the frosting reaches pourable consistency. Place matching pairs of whole and halved cookies on a wire rack over waxed paper. Pour icing over cookies; spread with a metal spatula to completely cover tops and sides of cookies. Let dry completely. Assemble and decorate as desired according to directions below.

TO MAKE A 4-SIDED TREE: Using a pastry bag fitted with a #5 round pastry tip, pipe green or white frosting to match the tree you are decorating. Pipe a line of frosting along the cut edge of 1 of the halved cookies; press frosted edge along center of a matching whole cookie. Let dry until firm. Stand up partially assembled tree. Attach a matching cookie half to the opposite side of the tree by piping frosting along the center of the whole cookie. Let dry completely. Decorate as desired.

TO MAKE AN 8-SIDED TREE: Assemble as described for a 4-sided tree, using white or green cookies. Using matching colored frosting, attach 4 more cookie halves; the halves should be a half-size smaller than the whole center cookie. Let dry completely. Decorate as desired.

TO MAKE CHRISTMAS LIGHTS DECORATION: Using a pastry bag fitted with a #2 round pastry tip, pipe cords with green frosting. Attach sprinkles for lights. Let dry completely.

TO MAKE SNOW-TIPPED DECORATION: Using a pastry bag fitted with a #8 round pastry tip, pipe snow on tips of branches with white frosting. Sprinkle with edible glitter. Let dry completely.

TO MAKE GARLAND DECORATION: Using a pastry bag fitted with a #21 star pastry tip, pipe garlands around trees with white or green frosting. Decorate with sprinkles if desired. Let dry completely.

1 FOUR-SIDED TREE: 181 cal., 5g fat (3g sat. fat), 25mg chol., 85mg sod., 31g carb. (21g sugars, 0 fiber), 2g pro.

ROYAL ICING RULES!
Take your cookie decorating to the next level with royal icing. What makes royal icing different from other glazes and frostings is that it hardens when cool, creating a candylike consistency. Meringue powder is the secret ingredient in royal icing. This egg white substitute helps the icing achieve its glossy consistency. You can buy meringue powder at grocery stores or online. As you're decorating cookies, keep the unused icing covered with a damp cloth to keep it from becoming hard. If needed, beat again on high speed to restore its texture.

Butterscotch Shortbread

After sampling these tender cookies in a specialty store, I knew
I had to duplicate them. My version has lots of toffee bits and
butterscotch chips. I give away dozens as home-baked gifts.
—*Sandy McKenzie, Braham, MN*

PREP: 30 MIN. + CHILLING • **BAKE:** 10 MIN./BATCH • **MAKES:** 4½ DOZEN

1 cup butter, softened
½ cup confectioners'
   sugar
1 tsp. vanilla extract
1¾ cups all-purpose flour
½ cup cornstarch
¼ tsp. salt
½ cup butterscotch chips,
   finely chopped
½ cup milk chocolate
   English toffee bits

1. In a large bowl, cream butter and confectioners' sugar until light and fluffy, 5-7 minutes. Beat in vanilla. Combine the flour, cornstarch and salt; gradually add to creamed mixture and mix well. Fold in butterscotch chips and toffee bits. Cover and refrigerate 1 hour or until easy to handle.

2. Preheat the oven to 350°. On a lightly floured surface, roll out dough to ¼-in. thickness. Cut with a floured 2-in. fluted round cookie cutter. Place 1 in. apart on ungreased baking sheets.

3. Bake for 10-12 minutes or until lightly browned. Remove to wire racks.

1 COOKIE: 76 cal., 5g fat (3g sat. fat), 10mg chol., 45mg sod., 8g carb. (1g sugars, 0 fiber), 1g pro. **DIABETIC EXCHANGES:** 1 fat, ½ starch.

Best-Ever Cutout Cookies

Nutmeg gives these tender cookies a special flavor.
You can use a variety of fun cutters to create a festive scene.
—*Christy Hinrichs, Parkville, MO*

PREP: 30 MIN. • **BAKE:** 10 MIN./BATCH + COOLING • **MAKES:** 4 DOZEN

1. Preheat oven to 375°. Cream butter, cream cheese and sugar until light and fluffy, 5-7 minutes. Beat in egg yolk and extracts. Combine flour, salt, baking soda and nutmeg; gradually add to creamed mixture. Cover and refrigerate until easy to handle, about 3 hours.

2. On a lightly floured surface, roll the dough to ⅛-in. thickness. Cut with floured 2½-in. cookie cutters. Place 1 in. apart on ungreased baking sheets. Bake until edges begin to brown, 8-10 minutes. Cool 2 minutes before removing from pans to wire racks to cool completely.

3. For icing, combine confectioners' sugar, water and meringue powder; beat on low speed just until blended. Beat on high until stiff peaks form, 4-5 minutes. Tint icing with food colors of your choice. Add additional water as needed to reach desired consistency. Using pastry bags and small round pastry tips, pipe designs on cookies as desired. Keep unused icing covered at all times with a damp cloth. If necessary, beat again on high speed to restore texture. Decorate with sprinkles and nonpareils if desired. Let iced cookies stand at room temperature several hours or until icing is dry and firm. Store in an airtight container.

1 **cup butter, softened**
3 **oz. cream cheese, softened**
1 **cup sugar**
1 **large egg yolk, room temperature**
½ **tsp. vanilla extract**
¼ **tsp. almond extract**
2¼ **cups all-purpose flour**
½ **tsp. salt**
¼ **tsp. baking soda**
⅛ **tsp. ground nutmeg**

ICING
3¾ **cups confectioners' sugar**
⅓ **cup water**
4 **tsp. meringue powder**
   Assorted gel food colors
   Sprinkles and nonpareils, optional

NOTE: Keep frosting thick to create texture for piping a tree; a #67 leaf tip works well! Thin frosting out with a little water for flooding. When layering frosting colors, let icing dry for at least an hour between layers.

1 FROSTED COOKIE: 116 cal., 5g fat (3g sat. fat), 16mg chol., 70mg sod., 18g carb. (13g sugars, 0 fiber), 1g pro.

Cherry-Filled Cookies

The luscious cherry filling peeking out of these rounds is just a hint of how scrumptious they are. Using a doughnut cutter to shape each cookie top really speeds up the process.
—*Delbert Benton, Guthrie Center, IA*

PREP: 25 MIN. + CHILLING • **BAKE:** 10 MIN./BATCH • **MAKES:** ABOUT 3 DOZEN

1. In a bowl, cream the shortening and sugars. Add eggs, buttermilk and vanilla; mix well. Combine flour, salt and baking soda; gradually add to creamed mixture and mix well. Cover and chill for 1 hour or until firm.

2. Divide dough in half. On a floured surface, roll each portion to ⅛-in. thickness. Cut with a 2¾-in. round cutter. Place half of the circles 2 in. apart on greased baking sheets; top each with a heaping teaspoon of pie filling. Cut holes in the center of remaining circles with a 1-in. round cutter; place over filled circles. Seal edges.

½	**cup shortening**
1	**cup packed brown sugar**
½	**cup sugar**
2	**large eggs, room temperature**
¼	**cup buttermilk**
1	**tsp. vanilla extract**
3½	**cups all-purpose flour**
½	**tsp. salt**
½	**tsp. baking soda**
1	**can (21 oz.) cherry pie filling**

3. Bake at 375° for 10 minutes or until golden brown. Cool on wire racks.

1 COOKIE: 125 cal., 3g fat (1g sat. fat), 10mg chol., 63mg sod., 22g carb. (12g sugars, 1g fiber), 2g pro.

Dutch Speculaas

These Dutch spice cookies taste similar to the windmill cookies we enjoy in the United States. In Holland, it's tradition to mold the dough into the shape of St. Nicholas and serve the baked cookies on Sinterklaas (St. Nicholas Day).
—Taste of Home *Test Kitchen*

PREP: 40 MIN. + CHILLING • **BAKE:** 10 MIN./BATCH • **MAKES:** ABOUT 2½ DOZEN

1 cup butter, softened
1 cup packed dark brown sugar
2 large eggs, room temperature
1 Tbsp. molasses
2 tsp. grated orange zest
3½ cups all-purpose flour
½ cup finely ground almonds
3 tsp. ground cinnamon
1 tsp. baking powder
½ tsp. ground nutmeg
½ tsp. ground cloves
¼ tsp. white pepper
¼ tsp. ground ginger
¼ tsp. ground cardamom

1. In a large bowl, cream butter and brown sugar until light and fluffy, 5-7 minutes. Beat in the eggs, molasses and orange zest. Combine the flour, ground almonds, cinnamon, baking powder, nutmeg, cloves, pepper, ginger and cardamom. Gradually add to creamed mixture and mix well. Cover and refrigerate for at least 4 hours or until easy to handle.

2. Preheat oven to 350°. On a parchment-lined surface, roll a small amount of dough to ⅛-in. thickness. Use a floured cookie stamp to press design into the dough, then cut with floured 3-in. cookie cutters, leaving 1 in. between cookies. Remove excess dough, and reroll scraps if desired.

3. Transfer parchment with dough to cookie sheet. If dough has warmed, place baking sheet in the refrigerator until it firms up, 10-15 minutes. Bake until the edges are lightly browned, 8-10 minutes. Remove from the pans to wire racks to cool.

1 COOKIE: 151 cal., 7g fat (4g sat. fat), 30mg chol., 65mg sod., 19g carb. (8g sugars, 1g fiber), 2g pro.

TO MAKE AHEAD: Dough can be made 2 days in advance. Let stand at room temperature for 30 minutes before rolling out. Cookies can be baked 1 week ahead of time and stored in an airtight container at room temperature or frozen for up to 1 month.

CHAPTER 2

Dreamy Drop Cookies

Sweet swap

Holiday Gumdrop Cookies

These cookies were my mother's special treat. They are perfect for keeping children busy—
kids can cut up the gumdrops and eat all the black ones so the dough doesn't turn gray.
—*Letah Chilston, Riverton, WY*

PREP: 15 MIN. + CHILLING • **BAKE:** 10 MIN./BATCH • **MAKES:** 4 DOZEN

1½ cups spice gumdrops
¾ cup coarsely chopped
  walnuts
½ cup golden raisins
1¾ cups all-purpose flour,
  divided
½ cup shortening
1 cup packed brown
  sugar
1 large egg, room
  temperature
¼ cup buttermilk
½ tsp. baking soda
½ tsp. salt

1. Cut gumdrops into small pieces; place in a bowl. Add walnuts, raisins and ¼ cup flour; toss to coat.

2. In a large bowl, beat the shortening and brown sugar until blended. Beat in egg, then buttermilk. In another bowl, whisk the remaining flour, baking soda and salt; gradually beat into shortening mixture. Stir in gumdrop mixture. Refrigerate, covered, 1 hour.

3. Preheat the oven to 375°. Drop the dough by rounded tablespoonfuls 2 in. apart onto ungreased baking sheets. Bake 8-10 minutes or until golden brown. Cool on pans 2 minutes. Remove to wire racks to cool.

1 COOKIE: 93 cal., 3g fat (1g sat. fat), 4mg chol., 46mg sod., 15g carb. (9g sugars, 0 fiber), 1g pro.

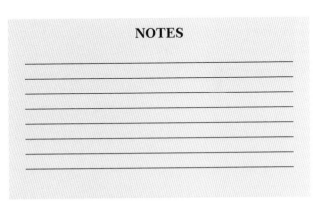

NOTES

White Chocolate Macadamia Cookies

White baking chips and macadamia nuts are a fantastic duo in these dreamy cookies. They are a nice change from the classic chocolate chip ones.
—*Cathy Lennon, Newport, TN*

PREP: 15 MIN. • BAKE: 10 MIN./BATCH + COOLING • MAKES: 2½ DOZEN

½ cup butter, softened
⅔ cup sugar
1 large egg, room temperature
1 tsp. vanilla extract
1 cup plus 2 Tbsp. all-purpose flour
½ tsp. baking soda
1 cup macadamia nuts, chopped
1 cup white baking chips

1. Preheat oven to 350°. In a large bowl, cream butter and sugar until light and fluffy, 5-7 minutes. Beat in the egg and vanilla. In another bowl, whisk flour and baking soda; gradually beat into creamed mixture. Stir in nuts and baking chips.

2. Drop by tablespoonfuls 2 in. apart onto ungreased baking sheets. Bake for 10-13 minutes or until golden brown. Cool on pans 1 minute. Remove to wire racks to cool completely.

1 COOKIE: 127 cal., 8g fat (4g sat. fat), 16mg chol., 69mg sod., 12g carb. (8g sugars, 1g fiber), 1g pro.

NUTTY FOR MACADAMIAS
Macadamia nuts are a popular snack nut, so you'll probably have lots of choices at the market—roasted, salted, even flavored. Any variety will work in baking; the biggest effect will be on the flavor of the finished baked good, which is entirely up to your own personal preference. Just keep in mind that this recipe does not contain any salt; if you're using unsalted raw nuts, you might want to add a little salt to bump up the flavor.

Buttery Potato Chip Cookies

Can't decide whether to bring chips or cookies to the tailgate? These crisp and buttery cookies make plenty for the crowd and will keep people guessing the secret ingredient.
—*Rachel Roberts, Lemoore, CA*

PREP: 15 MIN. • **BAKE:** 10 MIN./BATCH • **MAKES:** 4½ DOZEN

1. Preheat oven to 350°. In a large bowl, cream butter and sugar until light and fluffy, 5-7 minutes. Beat in vanilla. Gradually add flour to creamed mixture and mix well. Stir in potato chips and walnuts.

2. Drop mixture by rounded tablespoonfuls 2 in. apart onto ungreased baking sheets. Bake 10-12 minutes or until lightly browned. Cool 2 minutes before removing from pans to wire racks.

1 COOKIE: 126 cal., 9g fat (5g sat. fat), 18mg chol., 67mg sod., 11g carb. (4g sugars, 0 fiber), 1g pro.

2 cups butter, softened
1 cup sugar
1 tsp. vanilla extract
3½ cups all-purpose flour
2 cups crushed potato chips
¾ cup chopped walnuts

READER REVIEW

"Thought these were quite good. I would make sure to use the thicker-cut potato chips (with ridges), which help give the cookies more texture."
—WALKBAL, TASTEOFHOME.COM

Chocolate Macadamia Macaroons

This perfect macaroon has dark chocolate, chewy coconut and macadamia nuts and is dipped in chocolate—sinful and delicious!
—*Darlene Brenden, Salem, OR*

PREP: 20 MIN. • BAKE: 15 MIN. + COOLING • MAKES: 1½ DOZEN

2 cups sweetened shredded coconut
½ cup finely chopped macadamia nuts
⅓ cup sugar
3 Tbsp. baking cocoa
2 Tbsp. all-purpose flour
Pinch salt
2 large egg whites, lightly beaten
1 Tbsp. light corn syrup
1 tsp. vanilla extract
4 oz. semisweet chocolate, melted

1. Preheat oven to 325°. In a large bowl, mix the first 6 ingredients. Stir in egg whites, corn syrup and vanilla until blended.

2. Drop by tablespoonfuls 2 in. apart onto greased baking sheets. Bake until set and dry to the touch, 15-20 minutes. Cool on pans for 5 minutes. Remove cookies to wire racks to cool completely.

3. Dip half of each cookie into melted chocolate, allowing excess to drip off. Place on waxed paper and let stand until set.

1 COOKIE: 136 cal., 9g fat (5g sat. fat), 0 chol., 52mg sod., 15g carb. (11g sugars, 1g fiber), 2g pro.

Orange Cookies

Dozens of these citrusy delights travel along with me to the school and church functions I attend during the holidays. The abundant orange flavor is refreshing.
—*Diane Myers, Meridian, ID*

PREP: 20 MIN. • BAKE: 10 MIN./BATCH + COOLING • MAKES: 6 DOZEN

1 cup shortening
1½ cups sugar
1 cup buttermilk
3 large eggs, room temperature
⅔ cup orange juice
4½ tsp. grated orange zest
4 cups all-purpose flour
1 tsp. baking soda
1 tsp. baking powder

ICING
4¼ cups confectioners' sugar
¼ tsp. orange extract
⅓ to ½ cup orange juice

1. In a large bowl, cream shortening and sugar until light and fluffy, 5-7 minutes. Beat in buttermilk, eggs, orange juice and zest. Combine the dry ingredients; gradually add to the creamed mixture and mix well. Refrigerate dough for 20 minutes or until firm enough to handle.

2. Meanwhile, preheat the oven to 375°. Drop the dough by tablespoonfuls 2 in. apart onto ungreased baking sheets; bake until lightly browned, 8-10 minutes. Remove to wire racks to cool.

3. For icing, combine confectioners' sugar, orange extract and enough orange juice to achieve desired consistency. Drizzle or spread icing over cooled cookies.

1 COOKIE: 100 cal., 3g fat (1g sat. fat), 8mg chol., 34mg sod., 17g carb. (12g sugars, 0 fiber), 1g pro.

Chocolate Lebkuchen

Having lived in Germany, I try to keep my German cooking as authentic as possible. These lovely lebkuchen are a culinary Christmas custom.
—*Cathy Lemmon, Quinlan, TX*

PREP: 1 HOUR + COOLING • **BAKE:** 15 MIN. + COOLING • **MAKES:** ABOUT 1½ DOZEN

1 cup plus 2 Tbsp. all-purpose flour
¼ cup sugar
Dash salt
⅓ cup cold butter, cubed
3 Tbsp. water
1 tsp. vanilla extract

TOPPING
¼ cup butter, softened
¼ cup sugar
1 large egg, room temperature
1 Tbsp. canola oil
⅔ cup quick-cooking oats
½ cup all-purpose flour
⅓ cup ground almonds
⅓ cup ground hazelnuts
¼ cup baking cocoa
1 tsp. baking powder
½ tsp. ground cinnamon
¼ tsp. each ground cloves, cardamom and allspice
¼ cup finely chopped candied lemon peel
¼ cup finely chopped candied orange peel

GLAZE
6 oz. semisweet chocolate, chopped
2 oz. unsweetened chocolate, chopped
¼ cup butter, cubed

1. In a small bowl, combine the flour, sugar and salt; cut in butter until mixture resembles coarse crumbs. Combine water and vanilla; gradually add to crumb mixture, tossing with a fork until dough forms a ball.

2. On a lightly floured surface, roll out dough to ¹⁄₁₆-in. thickness. Cut with a floured 2½-in. round cookie cutter. Place on ungreased baking sheets. Bake at 325° until set, 8-10 minutes. Remove from pans to wire racks to cool.

3. For topping, in a small bowl, cream butter and sugar until light and fluffy, 5-7 minutes. Beat in the egg and oil. Combine the oats, flour, nuts, cocoa, baking powder and spices; gradually add to creamed mixture and mix well. Fold in candied peels.

4. Drop 1 rounded Tbsp. topping onto each cookie; gently press down. Place 2 in. apart on ungreased baking sheets. Bake at 325° until set, 13-16 minutes. Remove from pans to wire racks to cool.

5. In a microwave-safe bowl, melt chocolate and butter; stir until smooth. Dip each cookie halfway into chocolate; allow excess to drip off. Place on waxed paper; let stand until set. Store in airtight containers.

1 COOKIE: 238 cal., 14g fat (8g sat. fat), 32mg chol., 122mg sod., 27g carb. (15g sugars, 2g fiber), 4g pro.

Gingersnap Coconut Creams

When Christmas is around the corner, we love gingerbread cookies and macaroons.
I combine the two for a spiced gingersnap cookie with a coconut filling.
—*Darlene Brenden, Salem, OR*

PREP: 35 MIN. • **BAKE:** 10 MIN./BATCH + COOLING • **MAKES:** 4 DOZEN

1. Preheat oven to 375°. In a large bowl, cream butter and brown sugar until light and fluffy, 5-7 minutes. Beat in egg and molasses. In another bowl, whisk flour, baking soda and spices; gradually beat into creamed mixture.

2. Drop the dough by level teaspoonfuls 1 in. apart onto parchment-lined baking sheets. Bake for 6-8 minutes or just until edges begin to brown. Remove from pans to wire racks to cool completely.

3. For filling, in a small bowl, mix the butter, confectioners' sugar and extract until blended; stir in coconut. Spread on bottoms of half the cookies; cover with remaining cookies. If desired, dip edges of cookies in additional coconut.

1 SANDWICH COOKIE: 58 cal., 3g fat (2g sat. fat), 10mg chol., 50mg sod., 8g carb. (5g sugars, 0 fiber), 1g pro.

⅓ **cup butter, softened**
⅓ **cup packed brown sugar**
1 **large egg, room temperature**
⅓ **cup molasses**
1½ **cups all-purpose flour**
1 **tsp. baking soda**
½ **tsp. ground ginger**
½ **tsp. ground cinnamon**
¼ **tsp. ground cloves**

FILLING
¼ **cup butter, softened**
¾ **cup confectioners' sugar**
½ **tsp. orange extract**
¼ **cup sweetened shredded coconut**

Quick Cranberry Chip Cookies

I received these delightful cookies for Christmas a few years ago. I was watching my diet, but I couldn't stay away from them! The tart cranberries blend beautifully with the sweet chocolate and vanilla chips.
—*Jo Ann McCarthy, Canton, MA*

PREP: 25 MIN. • BAKE: 10 MIN./BATCH • MAKES: 6 DOZEN

- ½ cup butter, softened
- ½ cup shortening
- ¾ cup sugar
- ¾ cup packed brown sugar
- 2 large eggs, room temperature
- 1 tsp. vanilla extract
- 2¼ cups all-purpose flour
- 1 tsp. baking soda
- ½ tsp. salt
- 1 cup semisweet chocolate chips
- 1 cup white baking chips
- 1 cup dried cranberries
- 1 cup chopped pecans

1. Preheat oven to 375°. In a large bowl, cream butter, shortening and sugars until light and fluffy, 5-7 minutes. Add eggs, 1 at a time, beating well after each addition. Beat in vanilla. Combine flour, baking soda and salt; gradually add to the creamed mixture and mix well. Stir in chips, cranberries and pecans.

2. Drop by tablespoonfuls 2 in. apart onto ungreased baking sheets. Bake until golden brown, 9-11 minutes. Cool on pans 2 minutes before removing to wire racks to cool completely.

1 COOKIE: 97 cal., 5g fat (2g sat. fat), 10mg chol., 48mg sod., 12g carb. (8g sugars, 0 fiber), 1g pro.

CHOCOLATE NUT COOKIES: Omit semisweet chocolate chips, cranberries and pecans. Substitute 1 tsp. almond extract for the vanilla. Decrease the flour to 2 cups. Mix ¼ cup baking cocoa into the flour mixture. Stir in 1 cup chopped almonds with the white baking chips. Proceed as recipe directs.

CHOCOLATE-BUTTERSCOTCH CHIP COOKIES: Omit white baking chips, cranberries and pecans. Increase vanilla extract to 2 tsp. Increase semisweet chocolate chips to 2 cups and add 1 cup butterscotch chips. Proceed as recipe directs.

Stained Glass Cherry Macaroons

Macaroons have been around for ages. I wanted to keep
the true cookie but add a neat addition to a family favorite.
—Jamie Jones, Madison, GA

PREP: 45 MIN. • **BAKE:** 15 MIN./BATCH • **MAKES:** ABOUT 7 DOZEN

6 **large egg whites**
¾ **tsp. vanilla extract**
½ **tsp. salt**
¾ **cup sugar**
8 **cups sweetened
shredded coconut
(22 oz.)**
¾ **cup finely chopped
green candied cherries**
¾ **cup finely chopped red
candied cherries**
⅓ **cup all-purpose flour**

1. Place egg whites in a large bowl; let stand at room temperature 30 minutes.

2. Preheat oven to 325°. Add vanilla and salt to egg whites; beat on medium speed until foamy. Gradually add sugar, 1 Tbsp. at a time, beating on high after each addition until the sugar is dissolved. Continue beating until stiff glossy peaks form. In another bowl, combine coconut, cherries and flour; stir into egg white mixture.

3. Drop by tablespoonfuls 1 in. apart onto parchment-lined baking sheets. Bake for 14-16 minutes or until edges are golden. Cool on pans 2 minutes. Remove to wire racks to cool. Store in an airtight container.

FREEZE OPTION: Layer cookies between waxed paper in freezer containers. Freeze for up to 3 months. To use, thaw in covered containers.

1 COOKIE: 64 cal., 3g fat (3g sat. fat), 0 chol., 44mg sod., 9g carb. (8g sugars, 0 fiber), 1g pro.

Frosted Lemon-Ricotta Cookies

I work for a special education school and our students run their own catering business.
The students chose the lemon-ricotta cookies to submit as their favorite
cookie recipe. They say they are the yummiest and chewiest cookies ever!
Every time they make the cookies for a catering event, they get raves.
—*Renee Phillips, Owosso, MI*

PREP: 20 MIN. • BAKE: 10 MIN./BATCH + COOLING • MAKES: 3 DOZEN

1. Preheat oven to 375°. In a large bowl, beat butter and sugar until well blended, about 5 minutes. Beat in eggs, cheese, lemon juice and zest. Combine the flour, baking powder and salt; gradually add to the butter mixture and mix well.

2. Drop dough by heaping tablespoonfuls 3 in. apart onto greased baking sheets. Bake for 10-12 minutes or until lightly browned. Cool for 2 minutes before removing to wire racks to cool completely.

3. In a small bowl, combine frosting ingredients. Spread over cookies.

½ **cup butter, softened**
2 **cups sugar**
2 **large eggs,
room temperature,
lightly beaten**
1 **carton (15 oz.) ricotta
cheese**
3 **Tbsp. lemon juice**
1 **Tbsp. grated lemon
zest**
2½ **cups all-purpose flour**
1 **tsp. baking powder**
¾ **tsp. salt**

1 COOKIE: 139 cal., 4g fat (2g sat. fat), 22mg chol., 101mg sod., 24g carb. (17g sugars, 0 fiber), 3g pro.

SAVE THEM FOR A RAINY DAY
These lemon ricotta cookies last for 3-4 days at room temperature when stored in an airtight container. You can also freeze the unfrosted cookies for up to 3 months. Just store in a freezer container layered between waxed paper.

FROSTING
1½ **cups confectioners'
sugar**
3 **Tbsp. lemon juice**
2 **tsp. grated lemon zest**

Cocoa-Marshmallow Cookies

It was a childhood treat for me when Mom let me help her make these cookies. Nowadays, I always double the recipe because they disappear so fast. The marshmallow is a nice surprise under the sweet frosting.
—Lynell Renner, Zap, ND

PREP: 25 MIN. • BAKE: 10 MIN. • MAKES: 2½ DOZEN

1   **cup sugar**
½   **cup shortening**
1   **large egg, room temperature**
¼   **cup 2% milk**
1¾ **cups all-purpose flour**
½   **cup baking cocoa**
1   **tsp. baking soda**
½   **tsp. salt**
12 **large marshmallows, halved**

FROSTING
2   **cups confectioners' sugar**
2   **Tbsp. baking cocoa**
1   **Tbsp. butter, softened**
3   **to 4 Tbsp. 2% milk**

1. In a large bowl, cream sugar and shortening until light and fluffy, 5-7 minutes. Beat in egg and milk. Combine the flour, cocoa, baking soda and salt; add to the creamed mixture and mix well.

2. Drop by tablespoonfuls onto ungreased baking sheets. Bake at 350° for 8 minutes. Place half of a marshmallow on each cookie; bake 2 minutes longer.

3. Remove from oven and press marshmallows down with a fork. Cool. Meanwhile, for the frosting, in a large bowl, combine the confectioners' sugar, cocoa, butter and enough milk to reach desired consistency. Pipe onto cookies.

1 COOKIE: 119 cal., 3g fat (1g sat. fat), 6mg chol., 80mg sod., 22g carb. (15g sugars, 0 fiber), 1g pro.

Iced Oatmeal Apple Toffee Cookies

There's nothing quite like the classic iced oatmeal cookie, but when you add in toffee bits and apples, things get even better. To top these treats, drizzle each with a sweet cinnamon sugar glaze. Now that's what I call oatmeal cookie heaven.
—*Colleen Delawder, Herndon, VA*

PREP: 25 MIN. • BAKE: 10 MIN./BATCH + COOLING • MAKES: 6½ DOZEN

- 1 **cup unsalted butter, softened**
- ⅔ **cup sugar**
- ⅔ **cup packed light brown sugar**
- 2 **large eggs, room temperature**
- 3 **tsp. vanilla extract**
- 2 **cups all-purpose flour**
- 2 **cups quick-cooking oats**
- 2½ **tsp. ground cinnamon**
- 1 **tsp. kosher salt**
- 1 **tsp. baking soda**
- 1 **tsp. baking powder**
- 2 **medium apples, finely chopped**
- 1 **cup brickle toffee bits**

ICING
- 2 **cups confectioners' sugar**
- 3 **Tbsp. heavy whipping cream**
- 2 **Tbsp. water**
- 1 **tsp. ground cinnamon**

1. Preheat oven to 375°. In a large bowl, cream butter and sugars until light and fluffy, 5-7 minutes. Beat in eggs and vanilla. In another bowl, whisk the flour, oats, cinnamon, kosher salt, baking soda and baking powder; gradually beat into creamed mixture. Fold in apples and toffee bits.

2. Drop the dough by tablespoonfuls 2 in. apart onto parchment-lined baking sheets. Bake until golden brown, 10-12 minutes. Cool on pans 2 minutes before removing to wire racks to cool completely. Combine icing ingredients; drizzle over the cooled cookies. Let stand until set.

1 COOKIE: 89 cal., 4g fat (2g sat. fat), 13mg chol., 67mg sod., 13g carb. (9g sugars, 0 fiber), 1g pro.

Soft Buttermilk Sugar Cookies

My grandma used to make these soft, old-fashioned cookies.
The memory of her and these cookies go together!
—*Traci Rowlett, Oldenburg, IN*

PREP: 20 MIN. • **BAKE:** 10 MIN./BATCH • **MAKES:** ABOUT 2½ DOZEN

1. In a large bowl, cream shortening and 1 cup sugar until light and fluffy, 5-7 minutes. Beat in eggs and vanilla. Combine flour, baking powder, salt and baking soda; add to creamed mixture alternately with buttermilk, beating well after each addition (batter will be moist).

2. Combine cinnamon and remaining sugar. Drop dough by tablespoonfuls onto greased baking sheets. Sprinkle with cinnamon-sugar.

3. Bake at 375° until edges begin to brown, 8-10 minutes. Remove to wire racks. Store in an airtight container.

NOTE: To substitute for each cup of buttermilk, use 1 Tbsp. white vinegar or lemon juice plus enough milk to measure 1 cup. Stir, then let stand for 5 minutes. Or, use 1 cup plain yogurt or 1¾ tsp. cream of tartar plus 1 cup milk.

1 SERVING: 90 cal., 3g fat (1g sat. fat), 13mg chol., 123mg sod., 14g carb. (8g sugars, 0 fiber), 1g pro.

½ cup shortening
1¼ cups sugar, divided
2 large eggs, room temperature
2 tsp. vanilla extract
2 cups all-purpose flour
2 tsp. baking powder
1 tsp. salt
½ tsp. baking soda
½ cup buttermilk
¼ tsp. ground cinnamon

White Chocolate Pumpkin Dreams

If you like pumpkin pie, you'll love these delicious pumpkin cookies dotted with white chocolate chips and chopped pecans. Drizzled with a brown sugar icing, they're irresistible.
—*Jean Kleckner, Seattle, WA*

PREP: 25 MIN. • **BAKE:** 15 MIN./BATCH + COOLING • **MAKES:** 6½ DOZEN

1 cup butter, softened
½ cup sugar
½ cup packed
  brown sugar
1 large egg, room
  temperature
2 tsp. vanilla extract
1 cup canned pumpkin
2 cups all-purpose flour
3½ tsp. pumpkin pie spice
1 tsp. baking powder
1 tsp. baking soda
¼ tsp. salt
1 pkg. (10 to 12 oz.) white
  baking chips
1 cup chopped pecans

PENUCHE FROSTING
½ cup packed
  brown sugar
3 Tbsp. butter
¼ cup 2% milk
1½ to 2 cups confectioners'
  sugar

1. Preheat oven to 350°. In a large bowl, cream butter and sugars until light and fluffy, 5-7 minutes. Beat in the egg, vanilla and pumpkin. Combine dry ingredients; gradually add to the creamed mixture and mix well. Stir in the chips and pecans.

2. Drop by tablespoonfuls 2 in. apart onto ungreased baking sheets. Bake for 12-14 minutes or until firm. Remove to wire racks to cool.

3. For frosting, combine brown sugar and butter in a small saucepan. Bring to a boil; cook over medium heat until slightly thickened, about 1 minute. Cool for 10 minutes. Add the milk; beat until smooth. Beat in enough confectioners' sugar to reach the desired consistency. Spread over cooled cookies.

1 COOKIE: 93 cal., 5g fat (3g sat. fat), 11mg chol., 58mg sod., 12g carb. (9g sugars, 0 fiber), 1g pro.

READER REVIEW
"Wonderful! The only thing I might change would be to add raisins, but they're great without."
—BANDEMOM, TASTEOFHOME.COM

Bananas Foster Cookies

I was in a Christmas baking frenzy, trying to decide what to make next.
My roommate suggested something with bananas and walnuts, so I created
this recipe. Rolling the dough in brown sugar adds a nice caramel touch.
—*Elizabeth Smith, Arnold, PA*

PREP: 30 MIN. • BAKE: 10 MIN./BATCH • MAKES: ABOUT 5½ DOZEN

½ cup butter, softened
4 oz. cream cheese, softened
1 cup packed brown sugar
½ cup sugar
2 large eggs, room temperature
1 cup mashed ripe bananas (about 2 medium)
1 Tbsp. rum
2 tsp. vanilla extract
3 cups all-purpose flour
2 tsp. ground cinnamon
1½ tsp. baking powder
1 tsp. salt
1 tsp. baking soda
2 cups old-fashioned oats
1 cup chopped walnuts
½ cup packed brown sugar

1. Preheat oven to 350°. In a large bowl, cream butter, cream cheese and sugars until blended. Beat in eggs, bananas, rum and vanilla. In another bowl, whisk the flour, cinnamon, baking powder, salt and baking soda; gradually beat into creamed mixture. Stir in the oats and walnuts.

2. Shape rounded teaspoons of dough into balls; roll in additional brown sugar. Place 1 in. apart on ungreased baking sheets. Bake until the edges begin to brown, 10-12 minutes. Remove from pans to wire racks to cool. Store in airtight containers.

1 COOKIE: 85 cal., 4g fat (1g sat. fat), 11mg chol., 86mg sod., 12g carb. (5g sugars, 1g fiber), 2g pro.

NOTES

_____
_____
_____
_____
_____
_____
_____
_____

Sour Cream Date Drops

Sour cream lends the perfect tender consistency to these cookies filled with old-fashioned flavor. The recipe has earned me first prize at many fairs!
—*Carol Steiner, Arrowwood, AB*

PREP: 20 MIN. • **BAKE:** 10 MIN./BATCH • **MAKES:** 6 DOZEN

1. In a large bowl, cream butter and sugars until light and fluffy, 5-7 minutes. Beat in the eggs, sour cream and vanilla. Combine the flour, salt, cinnamon, baking soda and cloves; gradually add to creamed mixture and mix well. Stir in the dates, nuts and cherries.

2. Drop by tablespoonfuls 2 in. apart onto greased baking sheets. Bake at 375° for 10-12 minutes or until lightly browned. Remove to wire racks. Store in an airtight container with waxed paper between layers.

1 COOKIE: 77 cal., 3g fat (1g sat. fat), 11mg chol., 58mg sod., 11g carb. (7g sugars, 0 fiber), 1g pro.

½ cup butter, softened
1 cup packed brown sugar
½ cup sugar
2 large eggs, room temperature
1 cup sour cream
1 tsp. vanilla extract
2½ cups all-purpose flour
1 tsp. salt
1 tsp. ground cinnamon
½ tsp. baking soda
¼ tsp. ground cloves
1 cup finely chopped dates
1 cup chopped walnuts
1 cup candied cherries, chopped

Cran-Orange Cookies

A sweet orange frosting pairs well with the tart cranberry flavor in these soft, cakelike cookies.
—*Crystal Jo Bruns, Iliff, CO*

PREP: 30 MIN. • BAKE: 15 MIN./BATCH + COOLING • MAKES: 6 DOZEN

- 1 **cup butter, softened**
- 1 **cup sugar**
- ½ **cup packed brown sugar**
- 1 **large egg, room temperature**
- 2 **Tbsp. orange juice**
- 1 **tsp. grated orange zest**
- 2½ **cups all-purpose flour**
- ½ **tsp. salt**
- ½ **tsp. baking soda**
- 2 **cups chopped fresh or frozen cranberries**
- ½ **cup chopped walnuts**

ICING
- 1½ **cups confectioners' sugar**
- 2 **Tbsp. orange juice**
- ½ **tsp. grated orange zest**

1. In a large bowl, cream butter and sugars until light and fluffy, 5-7 minutes. Beat in egg, orange juice and zest. Combine flour, salt and baking soda; gradually add to the creamed mixture and mix well. Stir in cranberries and walnuts.

2. Drop by tablespoonfuls 2 in. apart onto greased baking sheets. Bake at 375° for 12-14 minutes or until edges are lightly browned. Remove to wire racks to cool.

3. Combine icing ingredients; spread over cooled cookies.

1 COOKIE: 73 cal., 3g fat (2g sat. fat), 9mg chol., 47mg sod., 11g carb. (7g sugars, 0 fiber), 1g pro.

Italian Toto Cookies

I think this cookie is the perfect combination of chocolate, orange and coffee flavors with a satisfying moist, dense texture.
—*Lilly Rudiy, Medina, OH*

PREP: 1½ HOURS • **BAKE** 10 MIN./BATCH • **MAKES:** ABOUT 10½ DOZEN

2 **Tbsp. instant espresso powder**
¼ **cup hot water**
1 **cup butter, softened**
¾ **cup sugar**
½ **cup packed light brown sugar**
3 **large eggs, room temperature**
3 **Tbsp. chocolate syrup**
4 **tsp. grated orange zest**
1 **tsp. orange extract**
1 **Tbsp. coffee liqueur, optional**
2 **tsp. coffee extract, optional**
1 **tsp. vanilla extract**
4½ **cups all-purpose flour**
½ **cup dark baking cocoa**
4 **tsp. baking powder**
1 **tsp. ground cinnamon**
½ **tsp. baking soda**
½ **tsp. ground allspice**
¼ **tsp. salt**
1 **cup finely chopped walnuts, toasted**
1 **cup (6 oz.) miniature semisweet chocolate chips**

GLAZE
1 **pkg. (2 lbs.) confectioners' sugar**
4 **tsp. grated orange zest**
¾ **to 1 cup orange juice**

1. Preheat the oven to 350°. In a small bowl, dissolve espresso powder in hot water; cool slightly. In a large bowl, cream the butter and sugars until light and fluffy, 5-7 minutes. Beat in eggs, then cooled espresso mixture, chocolate syrup, zest, orange extract, coffee liqueur and extract if desired, and vanilla (mixture will look curdled). In another bowl, whisk flour, baking cocoa, baking powder, cinnamon, baking soda, allspice and salt; gradually beat into creamed mixture. Stir in walnuts and chocolate chips. Refrigerate 30 minutes or until firm enough to roll.

2. Shape dough into 1-in. balls; place 2 in. apart on parchment-lined baking sheets. Bake until firm, 10-12 minutes.

3. Meanwhile, for glaze, in a large bowl, mix confectioners' sugar, zest and enough orange juice to reach a dipping consistency. Remove cookies from oven. Immediately dip cookies into glaze; allow the excess to drip off. Place on wire racks; let stand until set. Drizzle cookies with remaining glaze; let stand until set. Store between pieces of waxed paper in airtight containers.

1 COOKIE: 80 cal., 3g fat (1g sat. fat), 8mg chol., 38mg sod., 14g carb. (10g sugars, 0 fiber), 1g pro.

Hazelnut Dream Cookies

I sampled these goodies at a Bible study and knew from the first bite that I had to have the recipe. To my surprise, the rich cookies require just four ingredients.
—*Julie Peterson, Crofton, MD*

TAKES: 25 MIN. • MAKES: 2 DOZEN

1. Preheat oven to 350°. In a large bowl, beat Nutella, flour and egg until blended. Stir in hazelnuts.

2. Drop by tablespoonfuls 2 in. apart onto ungreased baking sheets. Bake until set, 8-10 minutes. Remove from pans to wire racks to cool.

1 COOKIE: 92 cal., 5g fat (1g sat. fat), 8mg chol., 8mg sod., 11g carb. (7g sugars, 1g fiber), 2g pro.

1   cup Nutella
⅔   cup all-purpose flour
1   large egg, room
    temperature
½   cup chopped hazelnuts

Marokanky (Czech Fruit Cookies)

These Czech cookies are crunchy on the outside and chewy on the inside. The batter is prepared on the stovetop, then cooled and baked. The original recipe calls for nuts and candied orange zest, but any dried fruit or combination of dried fruits can be used in place of the candied zest.
—*Cyndee Sindelar, Princeton, NJ*

PREP: 30 MIN. • **BAKE:** 10 MIN./BATCH • **MAKES:** ABOUT 1½ DOZEN

⅔ cup confectioners' sugar
2 Tbsp. all-purpose flour
½ cup heavy whipping cream
½ cup sliced almonds
¼ cup finely chopped walnuts
¼ cup chopped candied orange zest
¼ cup dried cranberries, chopped
1 tsp. vanilla extract
3 oz. bittersweet chocolate, chopped
1 tsp. shortening

1. Preheat oven to 350°. In a large saucepan, mix confectioners' sugar and flour. Whisk in cream. Cook and stir over medium heat until thickened and bubbly. Reduce heat to low; cook and stir 2 minutes longer.

2. Remove from heat. Stir in almonds, walnuts, orange zest, cranberries and vanilla. Cool completely.

3. Drop by tablespoonfuls onto parchment-lined baking sheets. Bake until edges begin to brown, 10-12 minutes. Cool on pans for 10 minutes. Remove to wire racks to cool completely.

4. In a microwave, melt chocolate and shortening; stir until smooth. Dip each cookie bottom into the chocolate; allow the excess to drip off. Place on waxed paper-lined baking sheets; refrigerate until set. Store between pieces of waxed paper in an airtight container.

1 COOKIE: 115 cal., 6g fat (3g sat. fat), 8mg chol., 18mg sod., 13g carb. (11g sugars, 1g fiber), 1g pro.

MORE CHOCOLATE, PLEASE!
Try dipping them into or drizzling them with chocolate—milk, semisweet, white or ruby— to put your own twist on these cookies.

Hot Chocolate Peppermint Cookies

This is a variation of the cookies my mother made when I was growing up, and now my teenage daughter and I bake them together. They're always a huge hit!
—*Larry Piklor, Johnsburg, IL*

PREP: 30 MIN. • **BAKE:** 10 MIN./BATCH + COOLING • **MAKES:** ABOUT 3½ DOZEN

1. Preheat oven to 375°. Cream butter and sugar in a large bowl until light and fluffy, 5-7 minutes. Beat in egg and extract. Combine flour, cocoa powder, salt and baking soda; gradually add to creamed mixture and mix well.

2. Drop by tablespoonfuls 2 in. apart onto greased baking sheets. Bake for 10-12 minutes or until tops are cracked. Remove to wire racks to cool completely.

3. In a microwave, melt the chocolate chips; stir until smooth. Drop a teaspoonful of marshmallow creme into the center of each cookie. Dip half of each cookie into the melted chocolate; allow the excess to drip off. Immediately sprinkle with candies. Place on waxed paper; let stand until set. Store in an airtight container.

1 COOKIE: 145 cal., 7g fat (4g sat. fat), 18mg chol., 132mg sod., 19g carb. (12g sugars, 1g fiber), 2g pro.

1   **cup butter, softened**
1   **cup sugar**
1   **large egg, room temperature**
1   **tsp. peppermint extract**
2⅓ **cups all-purpose flour**
⅓   **cup baking cocoa**
1   **tsp. salt**
1   **tsp. baking soda**
1   **pkg. (11½ oz.) milk chocolate chips**
1   **cup marshmallow creme**
1   **cup finely crushed peppermint candies**

Jeweled Coconut Drops

Red raspberry preserves add a festive flair to these tender coconut cookies.
Perfect for potlucks and cookie exchanges, the shaped goodies
never last long when I make them for my husband and two sons.
—*Ellen Marie Byler, Munfordville, KY*

PREP: 25 MIN. + CHILLING • **BAKE:** 10 MIN./BATCH + COOLING • **MAKES:** ABOUT 3½ DOZEN

1. Cream butter, cream cheese and sugar until light and fluffy, 5-7 minutes. Beat in egg yolk, orange juice and almond extract. In a separate bowl, whisk flour, baking powder and salt; gradually beat into creamed mixture. Stir in 3 cups coconut. Refrigerate until easy to handle, about 30 minutes.

2. Preheat the oven to 350°. Shape rounded tablespoons of dough into balls; roll in the remaining coconut. Place 2 in. apart on ungreased baking sheets. Press a deep indentation in the center of each cookie with the end of a wooden spoon handle. Bake until edges are light brown, 8-10 minutes. Cool for 1 minute. Using the wooden spoon, enlarge any indentations that may have narrowed or closed. Remove cookies from pans to wire racks. Fill with preserves; cool completely.

⅓ cup butter, softened
3 oz. cream cheese, softened
¾ cup sugar
1 large egg yolk, room temperature
2 tsp. orange juice
1 tsp. almond extract
1¼ cups all-purpose flour
1½ tsp. baking powder
¼ tsp. salt
3¾ cups sweetened shredded coconut, divided
1 cup seedless raspberry preserves, warmed

1 COOKIE: 110 cal., 5g fat (4g sat. fat), 10mg chol., 71mg sod., 16g carb. (12g sugars, 0 fiber), 1g pro.

HAVE FUN FILLING
The sky's the limit when it comes to filling coconut drops. Strawberry, apricot or cherry jams would work here, as would orange marmalade. Use store-bought or homemade lemon curd, or even pour in a little puddle of melted chocolate if you like. It won't have the same jeweled effect but will still be delicious!

CHAPTER #3
Shaped Cookies

Sour Cream Twists

The recipe for these tasty twists has been in my family for generations. I like to give them a festive look for the holidays by adding red or green colored sugar.
—*Kathy Floyd, Greenville, FL*

PREP: 30 MIN. • BAKE: 15 MIN./BATCH • MAKES: 8 DOZEN

1   pkg. (¼ oz.) active dry yeast
¼   cup warm water (110° to 115°)
4   cups all-purpose flour
¾   tsp. salt
½   cup cold butter, cubed
½   cup shortening
2   large eggs, room temperature, lightly beaten
½   cup sour cream
3   tsp. vanilla extract, divided
1½ cups sugar
    Red or green colored sugar

1. In a small bowl, dissolve yeast in water. Let stand for 5 minutes. In a large bowl, stir together flour and salt. Cut in butter and shortening until particles are the size of small peas. Stir in eggs, sour cream, 1 tsp. vanilla and the yeast mixture. Mix thoroughly (dough will be stiff and resemble pie pastry).

2. Combine white sugar and remaining vanilla; lightly sprinkle ½ cup over a pastry cloth. Roll out half of the dough on prepared pastry cloth into a rectangle. Sprinkle with about 1 Tbsp. of the sugar mixture plus some red or green colored sugar. Fold rectangle into thirds by folding 1 end of dough over center and folding other end over to make 3 layers.

3. Give dough a quarter turn and repeat rolling, sugaring and folding 2 more times. Roll out into a 16x9-in. rectangle. Cut into 3x1-in. strips. Twist each strip 2 or 3 times. Place strips on chilled ungreased baking sheets. Repeat with the remaining dough, sugar mixture and colored sugar.

4. Bake at 375° for 15-20 minutes or until light golden brown. Immediately remove cookies to wire racks.

1 COOKIE: 53 cal., 2g fat (1g sat. fat), 7mg chol., 28mg sod., 7g carb. (3g sugars, 0 fiber), 1g pro.

Roly-Poly Santas

Tuck these fanciful Santas onto every gift cookie
tray you make. They're guaranteed to be a hit!
—Andrew Syer, Oak Ridge, MO

PREP: 1 HOUR • BAKE: 15 MIN. + COOLING • MAKES: 1 DOZEN

1 cup butter, softened
½ cup sugar
1 Tbsp. 2% milk
1 tsp. vanilla extract
2¼ cups all-purpose flour
 Red paste food coloring

ICING
½ cup shortening
½ tsp. vanilla extract
2⅓ cups confectioners'
 sugar, divided
3 Tbsp. 2% milk, divided

ASSEMBLY
 Sanding sugar, sugar
 pearls and Red Hots

1. Preheat oven to 325°. In a large bowl, cream butter and sugar until light and fluffy, 5-7 minutes. Add milk and vanilla; mix well. Add flour and mix well. Remove 1⅔ cups dough; tint red. Shape white dough into 12 balls of ¾ in. each, 48 balls of ½ in. each and 12 balls of ¼ in. each. Shape red dough into 12 balls of 1¼ in. each and 60 balls of ½ in. each.

2. Place the 1¼ in. red balls on 2 ungreased baking sheets for the body of 12 Santas. Attach ¾-in. white balls for the heads. Attach four ½-in. red balls to each Santa for arms and legs. Attach ½ in. white balls to ends of arms and legs for hands and feet; lightly press together.

3. Shape remaining ½-in. red balls into hats. Attach ¼-in. white balls to tips of hats.

4. Bake until set, 12-15 minutes. Cool 10 minutes; carefully remove from pans to wire racks (cookies will be fragile).

5. For icing, combine shortening and vanilla in a small bowl; mix well. Gradually add 1⅓ cups confectioners' sugar; add 1 Tbsp. milk. Gradually add remaining sugar and milk.

6. Pipe a band of icing on hat, cuffs at hands and feet, and down the front and at bottom of jacket; while icing is still wet, sprinkle sugar over icing on brim of hat and cuffs at hands and feet. Pipe swirls of icing for beard and tip of hat. Place a Red Hot or a red sugar pearl for nose, black sugar pearls for eyes, and silver sugar pearls for buttons.

NOTE: The remaining dough may be shaped into balls and baked.

1 COOKIE: 422 cal., 24g fat (12g sat. fat), 41mg chol., 124mg sod., 50g carb. (32g sugars, 1g fiber), 3g pro.

Raspberry Almonettes

Sometimes that missing ingredient idea comes to me in my sleep, and I have to jot it down. The surprising filling in these cookies makes them fun to bake and even more fun to eat!
—*Angela Sheridan, Opdyke, IL*

PREP: 55 MIN. • **BAKE:** 10 MIN./BATCH + COOLING • **MAKES:** ABOUT 3½ DOZEN

1   cup butter, softened
2   cups sugar
2   large eggs, room temperature
1   cup canola oil
2   Tbsp. almond extract
4½ cups all-purpose flour
1   tsp. salt
1   tsp. baking powder
¾   cup sliced almonds, finely chopped

FILLING
1   pkg. (8 oz.) cream cheese, softened
½   cup confectioners' sugar
1   Tbsp. almond extract
¼   cup red raspberry preserves

1. Preheat oven to 350°. In a large bowl, cream butter and sugar until light and fluffy, 5-7 minutes. Add eggs, 1 at a time, beating well after each addition. Gradually beat in oil and extract. In another bowl, whisk flour, salt and baking powder; gradually beat into creamed mixture.

2. Shape the dough into 1-in. balls; press 1 side into the chopped almonds. Place 2 in. apart on ungreased baking sheets, almond side up. Flatten to ¼-in. thickness with bottom of a glass.

3. Bake for 8-10 minutes or until the edges are lightly browned. Cool cookies on pans for 5 minutes; remove to wire racks to cool completely.

4. For the filling, in a small bowl, beat cream cheese, confectioners' sugar and extract until smooth. Place rounded teaspoonfuls of filling on bottoms of half of the cookies. Make an indentation in center of each; fill with ¼ tsp. preserves. Cover with remaining cookies. Store in an airtight container in the refrigerator.

1 SANDWICH COOKIE: 216 cal., 13g fat (4g sat. fat), 26mg chol., 125mg sod., 23g carb. (12g sugars, 1g fiber), 2g pro.

White Chocolate-Cranberry Biscotti

The original version of this recipe was handed down from my great-aunt. Through the years, my mother and I have tried different flavor combinations, but this sweet and tart version has become a favorite.
—*Brenda Keith, Talent, OR*

PREP: 15 MIN. • BAKE: 35 MIN. + COOLING • MAKES: 2½ DOZEN

½ **cup butter, softened**
1 **cup sugar**
4 **large eggs, room temperature**
1 **tsp. vanilla extract**
3 **cups all-purpose flour**
1 **Tbsp. baking powder**
¾ **cup dried cranberries**
¾ **cup vanilla or white chips**

1. Preheat oven to 350°. In a large bowl, cream butter and sugar until light and fluffy, 5-7 minutes. Add eggs, 1 at a time, beating well after each addition. Beat in the vanilla. Combine the flour and baking powder; gradually add to creamed mixture and mix well. Stir in cranberries and vanilla chips. Divide dough into 3 portions.

2. On ungreased baking sheets, shape each portion into a 10x2-in. rectangle. Bake 20-25 minutes or until lightly browned. Cool for 5 minutes.

3. Transfer cookies to a cutting board; cut diagonally with a serrated knife into 1-in. slices. Place cut side down on ungreased baking sheets. Bake 15-20 minutes or until golden brown. Remove to wire racks to cool completely. Store in an airtight container.

1 COOKIE: 144 cal., 5g fat (3g sat. fat), 34mg chol., 86mg sod., 22g carb. (12g sugars, 1g fiber), 2g pro.

Italian Lemon Cookies

Christmas wouldn't be the same without my grandmother's cookies.
A plate full of these light and zesty cookies is divine!
—*Elisabeth Miller, Broadview Heights, OH*

PREP: 30 MIN. + CHILLING • **BAKE:** 15 MIN./BATCH • **MAKES:** 3 DOZEN

1 **cup butter, softened**
½ **cup sugar**
3 **large eggs, separated, room temperature**
2 **tsp. grated lemon zest**
2½ **cups all-purpose flour**
 Colored sugar

1. In a large bowl, cream the butter and sugar until light and fluffy, 5-7 minutes. Beat in egg yolks and lemon zest. Gradually beat in flour. Refrigerate, covered, 1 hour or until firm enough to shape.

2. Preheat oven to 350°. Shape level tablespoons of dough into 6-in. ropes. Shape each rope into an "S", then coil each end until it touches the center. Place 2 in. apart on ungreased baking sheets. Whisk the egg whites; brush over cookies. Sprinkle with colored sugar.

3. Bake until bottoms are brown, 12-14 minutes. Remove from pans to wire racks to cool.

1 COOKIE: 94 cal., 6g fat (3g sat. fat), 29mg chol., 47mg sod., 9g carb. (3g sugars, 0 fiber), 1g pro.

READER REVIEW
"I am very pleased with this recipe. The whole family enjoyed them. Forming the shapes was really easy. I'll be making these cookies all the time now."
—SYLVIAZAPATA-WEEDING, TASTEOFHOME.COM

Cuccidati

The compliments from family and friends make these Sicilian cookies worth the effort. It's the best recipe I've found!
—*Carolyn Fafinski, Dunkirk, NY*

PREP: 30 MIN. + CHILLING • **BAKE:** 10 MIN./BATCH + COOLING • **MAKES:** ABOUT 5 DOZEN

2 cups raisins
¾ lb. pitted dates
¾ cup sugar
2 small navel oranges, peeled and quartered
⅓ lb. dried figs
⅓ cup chopped walnuts
¼ cup water

DOUGH
1 cup shortening
1 cup sugar
2 large eggs, room temperature
¼ cup 2% milk
2 tsp. vanilla extract
3½ cups all-purpose flour
1 tsp. salt
1 tsp. baking powder
1 tsp. baking soda

GLAZE
2 cups confectioners' sugar
2 to 3 Tbsp. 2% milk

1. Place the first 7 ingredients in a food processor; cover and process until finely chopped. Set aside.

2. In a large bowl, cream shortening and sugar until light and fluffy, 5-7 minutes. Beat in the eggs, milk and vanilla. Combine the flour, salt, baking powder and baking soda; gradually add to creamed mixture and mix well. Divide dough into 4 portions; cover and refrigerate for 1 hour.

3. Preheat the oven to 400°. Roll out each portion between 2 sheets of waxed paper into a 16x6-in. rectangle. Spread 1 cup filling lengthwise down the center of each. Starting at a long side, fold the dough over the filling; fold the other side over the top. Pinch the seams and edges to seal. Cut each rectangle diagonally into 1-in. strips. Place seam side down on parchment-lined baking sheets.

4. Bake until edges are golden brown, 10-14 minutes. Cool for 10 minutes before removing from pans to wire racks to cool completely. Combine confectioners' sugar and enough milk to achieve desired consistency; drizzle over cookies. Store in an airtight container.

1 COOKIE: 132 cal., 4g fat (1g sat. fat), 7mg chol., 67mg sod., 24g carb. (17g sugars, 1g fiber), 1g pro.

PREP IN STEPS
The filling and dough for *cuccidati* can be made up to 3 days ahead of time. Break up the preparation time by making the filling 1 day and the dough on the next day. Then assemble the cookies on the third day.

Fudge-Filled Dessert Strips

This family favorite was handed down to me by my mother, and everyone who tastes the flaky chocolate-filled strips asks for the recipe. They're delicious!
—*Kimberly Santoro, Palm City, FL*

PREP: 40 MIN. + CHILLING • BAKE: 30 MIN./BATCH + COOLING • MAKES: 3 DOZEN

1 **cup butter, softened**
1 **pkg. (8 oz.) cream cheese, softened**
2 **cups all-purpose flour**
2 **cups semisweet chocolate chips**
1 **can (14 oz.) sweetened condensed milk**
2 **cups chopped walnuts Confectioners' sugar, optional**

1. In a large bowl, cream butter and cream cheese until light and fluffy, 3-4 minutes. Gradually add flour and mix well.

2. Turn onto lightly floured surface; knead until smooth, about 3 minutes. Divide dough into fourths; cover and refrigerate for 1-2 hours or until easy to handle.

3. In a microwave-safe bowl, melt the chocolate chips and milk; stir until smooth. Stir in the walnuts. Cool to room temperature.

4. Roll out each portion of dough onto an ungreased baking sheet into an 11x6½-in. rectangle. Spread ¾ cup chocolate filling down the center of each rectangle. Fold long sides to the center; press to seal all edges. Turn over so the seam sides are down.

5. Bake at 350° for 27-32 minutes or until lightly browned. Remove to wire racks to cool completely. Cut into ½-in. slices. Dust with confectioners' sugar if desired.

1 DESSERT STRIP: 214 cal., 15g fat (7g sat. fat), 24mg chol., 85mg sod., 18g carb. (12g sugars, 1g fiber), 4g pro.

Mini Baklava

Baklava provides amazing memories for me: My best friend made it for my bridal and baby showers. And then she taught me how to make it! These delicious little miniatures give you the taste of baklava in a bite-sized package.
—*Margaret Guillory, Eunice, LA*

PREP: 20 MIN. • BAKE: 10 MIN. + COOLING • MAKES: ABOUT 2½ DOZEN

½ **cup butter**
¼ **cup sugar**
1 **tsp. ground cinnamon**
1 **cup finely chopped pecans**
1 **cup finely chopped walnuts**
2 **pkg. (1.9 oz. each) frozen miniature phyllo tart shells**
Honey

1. Preheat oven to 350°. In a small saucepan over medium heat, melt the butter. Stir in the sugar and cinnamon. Bring to a boil. Reduce the heat; add the pecans and walnuts, tossing to coat. Simmer, uncovered, until nuts are lightly toasted, 5-10 minutes.

2. Place phyllo shells on a parchment-lined baking sheet. Spoon nut and butter sauce mixture evenly into shells. Bake until golden brown, 9-11 minutes. Cool completely on pan on a wire rack. Drizzle a drop of honey into each shell; let stand, covered, until serving. Serve with additional honey if desired.

1 FILLED PHYLLO CUP: 105 cal., 9g fat (2g sat. fat), 8mg chol., 33mg sod., 5g carb. (2g sugars, 1g fiber), 1g pro.

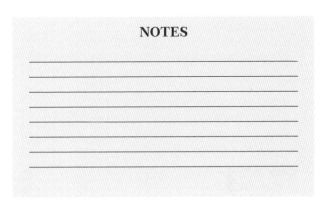

NOTES

Classic Candy Cane Butter Cookies

To make cookies that look like candy canes, color half the
dough in classic red and twist away. They're fun to hang on the
side of a coffee mug, or you can devour them all on their own.
—*Shannon Norris, Cudahy, WI*

PREP: 45 MIN. + CHILLING • **BAKE:** 10 MIN./BATCH + COOLING • **MAKES:** ABOUT 3 DOZEN

1 **cup butter, softened**
⅔ **cup sugar**
¼ **tsp. salt**
1 **large egg yolk, room
  temperature**
2 **tsp. vanilla extract**
2¼ **cups all-purpose flour
  Red paste food coloring**

1. In a large bowl, cream butter, sugar and salt until light
and fluffy, 5-7 minutes. Beat in the egg yolk and vanilla;
gradually beat in the flour. Divide dough in half; mix food
coloring into 1 half. Roll each dough portion into a 6-in.
square. Cover and refrigerate at least 1 hour or overnight.

2. Preheat oven to 350°. Cut each dough into 36 squares.
Working with a quarter of the dough at a time, keep the
remaining dough refrigerated. Roll 1 piece of plain dough
into a 6-in. rope; roll 1 piece of red dough into a 6-in. rope.
Place the ropes side by side. Lift left rope over the right;
repeat to form a twist. Repeat with the remaining dough.
Curving top of each twist to form hook of cane, place
1 in. apart on parchment-lined baking sheets.

3. Bake 7-9 minutes or until set. Cool on pans 3 minutes.
Remove to wire racks to cool completely.

1 COOKIE: 90 cal., 5g fat (3g sat. fat), 19mg chol., 57mg sod.,
10g carb. (4g sugars, 0 fiber), 1g pro.

Chocolate Snowballs

This is my favorite Christmas cookie recipe. The cookies remind me of the snowballs I packed as a child during many cold Wisconsin winters.
—*Dee Derezinski, Waukesha, WI*

PREP: 30 MIN. • **BAKE:** 15 MIN./BATCH + COOLING • **MAKES:** ABOUT 4 DOZEN

1. Preheat oven to 350°. In a large bowl, cream butter, sugar and salt until light and fluffy, 5-7 minutes. Beat in egg and vanilla. Gradually beat in flour. Stir in pecans and chocolate chips.

2. Shape the dough into 1-in. balls; place 2 in. apart on ungreased baking sheets. Bake until set and bottoms are lightly browned, 15-20 minutes. Cool on pans 2 minutes. Roll the warm cookies in the confectioners' sugar. Cool completely on wire racks. If desired, reroll cookies in confectioners' sugar.

¾ cup butter, softened
½ cup sugar
½ tsp. salt
1 large egg, room temperature
2 tsp. vanilla extract
2 cups all-purpose flour
1 cup chopped pecans or walnuts
1 cup (6 oz.) chocolate chips
Confectioners' sugar

1 COOKIE: 92 cal., 6g fat (3g sat. fat), 12mg chol., 49mg sod., 10g carb. (5g sugars, 1g fiber), 1g pro.

HERE'S A NUTTY IDEA!
We like pecans and walnuts, but you can substitute chopped pistachios, macadamia nuts or even almonds. Not a nut fan? Omit them entirely and add a few more chocolate chips!

Nutmeg Sugar Cookies

Autumn is one of my favorite times of the year because I love to bake.
These are one of my most-asked-about cookies. They always disappear fast.
—*Jean Wysocki, Westminster, CO*

PREP: 40 MIN. • BAKE: 10 MIN./BATCH + COOLING • MAKES: 7 DOZEN

1 cup butter, softened
¾ cup sugar
1 large egg, room
  temperature
2 tsp. vanilla extract
3 cups all-purpose flour
1 tsp. ground nutmeg
¼ tsp. salt

FROSTING
⅓ cup butter, softened
2 cups confectioners'
  sugar
1 tsp. rum extract
1 tsp. vanilla extract
2 to 3 Tbsp. half-and-half
  cream
  Ground nutmeg

1. In a large bowl, cream butter and sugar until light and fluffy, 5-7 minutes. Beat in egg and vanilla. Combine the flour, nutmeg and salt; gradually add to creamed mixture and mix well.

2. Divide dough into 14 pieces. Shape each portion into a 12-in. x ½-in.-thick rope. Cut ropes into 2-in. pieces. Place 2 in. apart on greased baking sheets.

3. Bake at 350° for 9-12 minutes or until set and bottoms are lightly browned. Cool for 1 minute before removing to wire racks to cool completely.

4. For frosting, in a small bowl, beat butter until fluffy. Add confectioners' sugar and extracts; beat until blended. Beat in enough cream to achieve desired consistency.

5. Frost cookies. Sprinkle with nutmeg. Store in an airtight container in the refrigerator.

1 COOKIE: 62 cal., 3g fat (2g sat. fat), 10mg chol., 29mg sod., 8g carb. (5g sugars, 0 fiber), 1g pro.

Jamaican Chocolate Cookies with Caramel Creme

I made these for an office party cookie contest—and not a crumb was left on the platter! Sweet potatoes are the secret ingredient. Canned sweet potatoes will work, too, if you're short on time.
—*Noelle Myers, Grand Forks, ND*

PREP: 45 MIN. + STANDING • **BAKE:** 10 MIN./BATCH + COOLING
MAKES: ABOUT 2½ DOZEN

1 **pkg. (11½ oz.) semisweet chocolate chunks, divided**
½ **cup butter, softened**
½ **cup confectioners' sugar**
½ **cup mashed sweet potatoes**
1 **tsp. minced fresh gingerroot**
½ **tsp. vanilla extract**
1¼ **cups all-purpose flour**
¼ **cup cornstarch**
2 **Tbsp. baking cocoa**
1½ **tsp. baking powder**
¼ **tsp. baking soda**
¼ **tsp. salt**

FILLING
⅔ **cup whipped cream cheese**
⅓ **cup dulce de leche**
2 **Tbsp. sweetened condensed milk**
⅛ **tsp. ground cinnamon**
⅛ **tsp. ground allspice**
⅛ **tsp. salt**

1. Preheat the oven to 375°. In a microwave, melt ⅔ cup chocolate chunks; stir until smooth. Cool slightly. In a large bowl, cream butter and confectioners' sugar until light and fluffy, 3-4 minutes. Beat in the sweet potatoes, cooled melted chocolate, ginger and vanilla. In another bowl, whisk the flour, cornstarch, baking cocoa, baking powder, baking soda and salt; gradually beat into creamed mixture.

2. Shape dough into ¾-in. balls; place 2½ in. apart on parchment-lined baking sheets. Flatten slightly with bottom of a glass dipped in confectioners' sugar. Bake until edges are firm, 8-10 minutes. Remove from pans to wire racks to cool completely.

3. Meanwhile, mix the filling ingredients until smooth. Spread filling on bottoms of half the cookies; cover with remaining cookies.

4. For chocolate coating, microwave remaining chocolate chunks; stir until smooth. Dip the cookies halfway into chocolate or drizzle chocolate over tops of cookies; let stand until set. Store between pieces of waxed paper in an airtight container in the refrigerator.

1 SANDWICH COOKIE: 134 cal., 7g fat (5g sat. fat), 12mg chol., 103mg sod., 17g carb. (10g sugars, 1g fiber), 2g pro.

Lacy Brandy Snaps

These cream-filled crisps are the perfect sweet treat. Include them on a holiday cookie plate or serve at the end of the meal with coffee or tea.
—*Natalie Bremson, Plantation, FL*

PREP: 30 MIN. • **BAKE:** 10 MIN./BATCH + COOLING • **MAKES:** 4 DOZEN

6 **Tbsp. unsalted butter, cubed**
⅓ **cup sugar**
3 **Tbsp. light corn syrup**
⅔ **cup all-purpose flour**
2 **tsp. brandy**
1 **tsp. ground ginger**

FILLING
4 **cups heavy whipping cream**
1¾ **cups confectioners' sugar**
½ **cup brandy**
Grated chocolate, optional

1. Preheat oven to 350°. In a small saucepan, combine the butter, sugar and corn syrup. Cook and stir over medium heat until butter is melted. Remove from the heat. Stir in the flour, brandy and ginger.

2. Drop by teaspoonfuls, 3 at a time, 3 in. apart onto a parchment-lined baking sheet. Bake until golden brown, 7-8 minutes.

3. Cool for 30-45 seconds. Working quickly, loosen each cookie and curl around a thick wooden spoon handle. (If the cookies become too cool to shape, return to the oven for 1 minute to soften.) Remove to wire rack to cool completely.

4. For filling, in a large bowl, beat cream until it begins to thicken. Add confectioners' sugar and brandy; beat until stiff peaks form. Just before serving, pipe cream mixture into cookies. Sprinkle ends with chocolate if desired.

1 COOKIE: 119 cal., 9g fat (5g sat. fat), 31mg chol., 9mg sod., 9g carb. (6g sugars, 0 fiber), 1g pro.

Lemon Anise Biscotti

With the growing popularity of gourmet coffees, cappuccino and espresso,
I'm finding lots of people enjoy these classic Sicilian dipping cookies.
—*Carrie Sherrill, Forestville, WI*

PREP: 25 MIN. • BAKE: 40 MIN. + COOLING • MAKES: 3 DOZEN

1. Preheat oven to 350°. In a small bowl, beat eggs and sugar for 2 minutes or until thickened. Add the oil and extracts; mix well. Combine flour, baking powder and salt; beat into egg mixture. Beat in lemon zest and aniseed.

2. Divide dough in half. On a lightly floured surface, shape each portion into a 12x2-in. rectangle. Transfer to a baking sheet lined with parchment. Flatten to ½-in. thickness.

3. Bake 30-35 minutes or until golden and tops begin to crack. Carefully remove to wire racks; cool for 5 minutes.

4. Transfer to a cutting board; cut with a serrated knife into scant ¾-in. slices. Place cut side down on ungreased baking sheets. Bake 5 minutes. Turn and bake until firm and golden brown, 5-7 minutes. Remove to wire racks to cool completely. If using glaze, whisk confectioners' sugar and lemon juice in a small bowl. Drizzle over biscotti; sprinkle with zest. Store in an airtight container.

1 COOKIE: 65 cal., 2g fat (0 sat. fat), 10mg chol., 50mg sod., 11g carb. (6g sugars, 0 fiber), 1g pro.

2 **large eggs**
1 **cup sugar**
¼ **cup canola oil**
½ **tsp. lemon extract**
¼ **tsp. vanilla extract**
2 **cups all-purpose flour**
1 **tsp. baking powder**
½ **tsp. salt**
4 **tsp. grated lemon zest**
2 **tsp. aniseed, crushed**

OPTIONAL GLAZE:
2 **cups confectioners' sugar**
3 **to 4 Tbsp. lemon juice**
   Grated lemon zest

A GREATER GLAZE
If you want your glaze a little thicker, whisk in more confectioners' sugar, a tablespoon at a time, until the desired consistency is reached. For a thinner glaze, gradually stir in a bit more lemon juice.

Raspberry Pastry Twists

Give regular round cookies a tasty twist with this recipe.
Feel free to replace the raspberry filling with cherry or almond.
—Taste of Home *Test Kitchen*

PREP: 40 MIN. + CHILLING • BAKE: 15 MIN./BATCH • MAKES: 32 COOKIES

1 **pkg. (8 oz.) cream cheese, softened**
½ **cup butter, softened**
2 **large egg yolks, room temperature**
2½ **cups all-purpose flour**
¾ **cup confectioners' sugar**
¼ **tsp. salt**
6 **Tbsp. raspberry cake and pastry filling, divided**
2 **Tbsp. 2% milk, optional**
  Coarse sugar, optional

1. In a large bowl, beat cream cheese and butter until fluffy. Beat in egg yolks. In another bowl, mix the flour, confectioners' sugar and salt; gradually add to cream cheese mixture. Divide dough in half. Shape each into a disk; cover and refrigerate overnight.

2. Remove from the refrigerator 1 hour before rolling. On a lightly floured surface, roll 1 portion of dough into a 12x8-in. rectangle. Spread 3 Tbsp. filling widthwise over half of the dough. Fold dough in half over the filling. Cut widthwise into sixteen ½-in. strips. Twist each strip 3 times; pinch unfolded ends to seal.

3. Place on parchment-lined baking sheets. If desired, lightly brush tops with milk and sprinkle with coarse sugar. Repeat with remaining dough and filling. Bake at 375° for 15-17 minutes or until bottoms are golden brown. Remove from pans to wire racks to cool.

1 COOKIE: 103 cal., 6g fat (4g sat. fat), 31mg chol., 56mg sod., 10g carb. (1g sugars, 0 fiber), 2g pro.

Peppermint Meltaways

This recipe is very pretty and looks festive on a cookie tray. I often put these meltaways in bright holiday containers to give to family and friends. And yes, they really do melt in your mouth!
—*Denise Wheeler, Newaygo, MI*

PREP: 30 MIN. + CHILLING • **BAKE:** 10 MIN./BATCH + COOLING • **MAKES:** ABOUT 2½ DOZEN

---

1 **cup butter, softened**
½ **cup confectioners' sugar**
½ **tsp. peppermint extract**
1¼ **cups all-purpose flour**
½ **cup cornstarch**

FROSTING
2 **Tbsp. butter, softened**
2 **Tbsp. 2% milk**
¼ **tsp. peppermint extract**
2 **to 3 drops red food coloring, optional**
1½ **cups confectioners' sugar**
½ **cup crushed peppermint candies**

1. In a small bowl, cream butter and confectioners' sugar until light and fluffy, 3-4 minutes. Beat in the extract. In another bowl, whisk flour and cornstarch; gradually beat into creamed mixture. Refrigerate, covered, 30 minutes or until firm enough to handle.

2. Preheat oven to 350°. Shape dough into 1-in. balls; place 2 in. apart on ungreased baking sheets. Bake 9-11 minutes or until bottoms are light brown. Remove from the pans to wire racks to cool completely.

3. In a small bowl, beat butter until creamy. Beat in milk, extract and, if desired, food coloring. Gradually beat in confectioners' sugar until smooth. Spread over cookies; sprinkle with candies. Store in an airtight container.

1 COOKIE: 126 cal., 7g fat (4g sat. fat), 18mg chol., 56mg sod., 15g carb. (9g sugars, 0 fiber), 1g pro.

Cherry Cheese Windmills

These pretty cookies look fancy, but they are really not much work. They're perfect for any occasion.
—*Helen McGibbon, Downers Grove, IL*

PREP: 25 MIN. + CHILLING • **BAKE:** 10 MIN./BATCH + COOLING • **MAKES:** ABOUT 2½ DOZEN

⅓ **cup butter, softened**
⅓ **cup shortening**
¾ **cup sugar**
1 **large egg, room temperature**
1 **Tbsp. 2% milk**
1 **tsp. vanilla extract**
2 **cups all-purpose flour**
1½ **tsp. baking powder**
¼ **tsp. salt**

FILLING
3 **oz. cream cheese, softened**
¼ **cup sugar**
¼ **tsp. almond extract**
½ **cup finely chopped maraschino cherries**
¼ **cup sliced almonds, toasted and chopped**

1. In a large bowl, cream the butter, shortening and sugar until light and fluffy, 5-7 minutes. Beat in the egg, milk and vanilla. In another bowl, combine the flour, baking powder and salt; gradually add to creamed mixture and mix well. Divide dough in half. Cover and refrigerate for 3 hours or until easy to handle.

2. In a small bowl, beat cream cheese, sugar and extract until smooth. Fold in cherries. On a floured surface, roll each portion of dough into a 10-in. square. With a sharp knife or pastry wheel, cut into 2½-in. squares. Place 2 in. apart on ungreased baking sheets. Make 1-in. cuts from each corner toward the center of the dough.

3. Drop teaspoonfuls of filling in the center of each square; sprinkle with the almonds. Fold alternating points to the center to form a windmill; moisten points with water and pinch gently at center to seal. Bake at 350° 8-10 minutes or until set. Move to wire racks to cool completely.

1 COOKIE: 126 cal., 6g fat (3g sat. fat), 16mg chol., 73mg sod., 15g carb. (8g sugars, 0 fiber), 1g pro.

Chai Snickerdoodles

When I think of winter, I think of two things: warm cookies and a cup of chai.
My recipe combines them in my favorite cookie—snickerdoodles!
—*Evangeline Bradford, Covington, KY*

PREP: 30 MIN. • BAKE: 10 MIN./BATCH • MAKES: 6½ DOZEN

2 **cups sugar**
2 **tsp. ground cinnamon**
1 **tsp. ground ginger**
1 **tsp. ground cardamom**
½ **tsp. ground allspice**
1 **cup butter, softened**
2 **large eggs, room temperature**
1½ **tsp. vanilla extract**
2¾ **cups all-purpose flour**
2 **tsp. cream of tartar**
1 **tsp. baking soda**
⅛ **tsp. salt**

1. In a small bowl, combine the sugar, cinnamon, ginger, cardamom and allspice. Remove ½ cup sugar mixture to a shallow bowl; set aside.

2. In a large bowl, cream butter and the remaining sugar mixture until light and fluffy, 5-7 minutes. Beat in eggs and vanilla extract. Combine the flour, cream of tartar, baking soda and salt; gradually add to creamed mixture and mix well.

3. Shape into 1½-in. balls; roll in reserved sugar mixture. Place 2 in. apart on parchment-lined baking sheets. Bake at 350° for 10-13 minutes or until edges begin to brown. Cool 2 minutes before removing from pans to wire racks.

1 COOKIE: 59 cal., 3g fat (2g sat. fat), 12mg chol., 38mg sod., 9g carb. (5g sugars, 0 fiber), 1g pro.

Chocolate Thumbprint Cookies

My group of friends had a weekly movie night during winters on Martha's Vineyard, and we'd take turns making a chocolate treat to share. These terrific cookies were an instant success. Once they debuted, I had to make them many more times.
—*Laura Bryant German, West Warren, MA*

PREP: 25 MIN. + CHILLING • **BAKE:** 10 MIN. + COOLING • **MAKES:** ABOUT 2½ DOZEN

1. In a large bowl, cream butter and sugar until light and fluffy, 5-7 minutes. Beat in the egg yolk, milk and vanilla. Combine flour, cocoa and salt; gradually add to creamed mixture and mix well. Cover and refrigerate until easy to handle, about 1 hour.

2. Preheat oven to 350°. In a small bowl, whisk egg white until foamy. Shape dough into 1-in. balls; dip in egg white, then roll in nuts. Place on greased baking sheets. Using a wooden spoon handle, make an indentation in center of each cookie. Bake until center is set, 10-12 minutes.

3. For filling, combine confectioners' sugar, butter, milk and vanilla; stir until smooth. Spoon or pipe ¼ tsp. into each warm cookie; gently press a chocolate kiss in the center. Carefully remove from pans to wire racks to cool completely.

1 COOKIE: 117 cal., 7g fat (3g sat. fat), 16mg chol., 52mg sod., 13g carb. (8g sugars, 1g fiber), 2g pro.

½ **cup butter, softened**
⅔ **cup sugar**
1 **large egg, separated, room temperature**
2 **Tbsp. 2% milk**
1 **tsp. vanilla extract**
1 **cup all-purpose flour**
⅓ **cup baking cocoa**
¼ **tsp. salt**
1 **cup finely chopped walnuts**

FILLING
½ **cup confectioners' sugar**
1 **Tbsp. butter, softened**
2 **tsp. 2% milk**
¼ **tsp. vanilla extract**
24 **milk chocolate kisses**

PREVENT CRACKED COOKIES
Using a gentle touch when imprinting the cookies with the spoon handle or your thumb will prevent the dough from cracking. If you still get a crack, gently reshape the cookie by pressing it toward the center. Because these cookies get a coating of chopped nuts, any remaining cracks should go unnoticed.

English Tea Cakes

These unique cookies are baked in muffin cups, giving them a perfectly round shape. I sometimes omit the pecans and decorate for holidays.
—*Beverly Christian, Fort Worth, TX*

PREP: 15 MIN. • **BAKE:** 10 MIN./BATCH • **MAKES:** 5 DOZEN

1. In a large bowl, cream butter and sugar until light and fluffy, 5-7 minutes. Beat in vanilla. Gradually add flour and mix well. Drop by heaping tablespoonfuls into greased miniature muffin cups; flatten slightly. Press a walnut half into the center of each.

2. Bake at 350° for 10-12 minutes or until edges are lightly browned. Cool for 2 minutes before removing from pans to wire racks.

1 TEA CAKE: 108 cal., 7g fat (4g sat. fat), 16mg chol., 49mg sod., 10g carb. (3g sugars, 0 fiber), 1g pro.

2 cups butter, softened
1 cup sugar
2 tsp. vanilla extract
4 cups all-purpose flour
60 walnut or pecan halves, toasted

READER REVIEW

"These cookies are easy and incredibly delicious. They disappear fast and melt in your mouth!"
—KIMELN, TASTEOFHOME.COM

Glazed Cherry Bonbon Cookies

You'll see these red and green bonbon cookies in my home every Yuletide. They're a standard on my cookie tray.
—Lori Daniels, Beverly, WV

PREP: 20 MIN. • BAKE: 15 MIN./BATCH + COOLING • MAKES: 3 DOZEN

- 36 **maraschino cherries**
- 1 **cup butter, softened**
- 1½ **cups confectioners' sugar**
- 1 **Tbsp. 2% milk**
- 3 **tsp. vanilla extract**
- 2¾ **cups all-purpose flour**
- ¼ **tsp. salt**

CHRISTMAS GLAZE
- 1¼ **cups confectioners' sugar**
- 1 **to 2 Tbsp. water**
  Red and green liquid food coloring
  Colored sprinkles

CHOCOLATE GLAZE
- 1 **oz. unsweetened chocolate, melted**
- 1 **tsp. vanilla extract**
- 1 **cup confectioners' sugar**
- 1 **to 2 Tbsp. water**
- ½ **cup chopped pecans or walnuts**

1. Pat cherries dry with paper towels; set aside. In a large bowl, cream butter and confectioners' sugar until light and fluffy, 3-4 minutes. Beat in milk and vanilla. Combine flour and salt; gradually add to creamed mixture and mix well.

2. Shape a tablespoonful of dough around each cherry, forming a ball. Place 2 in. apart on ungreased baking sheets. Bake at 350° for 14-16 minutes or until bottoms are browned. Remove to wire racks to cool.

3. For the Christmas glaze, in a small bowl, combine the confectioners' sugar and enough water to achieve a dipping consistency. Transfer half of the glaze to another bowl; tint 1 bowl green and the other red. Dip the tops of 9 cookies in green glaze and 9 cookies in red glaze, then decorate with sprinkles. Let stand until set.

4. For the chocolate glaze, in a small bowl, combine the confectioners' sugar and enough water to achieve dipping consistency. Stir in chocolate and vanilla. Dip the tops of remaining cookies in glaze, then sprinkle with nuts. Let stand until set.

1 COOKIE: 155 cal., 7g fat (4g sat. fat), 13mg chol., 53mg sod., 23g carb. (15g sugars, 1g fiber), 1g pro.

Orange Gingerbread Tassies

I make big Christmas cookie plates every year, and it's fun to include something with a different shape. These have a delicious flavor with the gingerbread and orange, and they are really easy! This is also yummy with lemon zest if you prefer that over the orange. You can decorate with some candied orange peel if you have it.

—Elisabeth Larsen, Pleasant Grove, UT

PREP: 20 MIN. + CHILLING • **BAKE:** 15 MIN. + COOLING • **MAKES:** 2 DOZEN

1. In a large bowl, beat first 7 ingredients until light and fluffy, 3-4 minutes. Gradually beat in flour. Refrigerate, covered, until firm enough to shape, about 1 hour.

2. Preheat oven to 350°. Shape dough into twenty-four 1-in. balls; press evenly onto bottoms and up sides of ungreased mini-muffin cups. Bake until golden brown, 15-18 minutes. Press centers with the handle of a wooden spoon to reshape as necessary. Cool completely in pan before removing to wire rack.

3. In a microwave-safe bowl, heat baking chips, cream and butter until blended, stirring occasionally. Stir in orange zest; cool completely. Spoon into crusts. Refrigerate until filling is soft-set. If desired, garnish with orange peel.

½ cup butter, softened
4 oz. cream cheese, softened
¼ cup molasses
1 tsp. ground ginger
½ tsp. ground cinnamon
½ tsp. ground allspice
¼ tsp. ground cloves
1 cup all-purpose flour
½ cup white baking chips
¼ cup heavy whipping cream
2 Tbsp. butter
4 tsp. grated orange zest
   Candied orange peel, optional

1 COOKIE: 91 cal., 6g fat (4g sat. fat), 13mg chol., 43mg sod., 9g carb. (5g sugars, 0 fiber), 1g pro.

Dipped Gingersnaps

I get a great deal of satisfaction making and giving time-tested treats like these soft, chewy cookies. Dipping them in white chocolate makes great gingersnaps even more special.
—*Laura Kimball, West Jordan, UT*

PREP: 20 MIN. • BAKE: 10 MIN./BATCH + COOLING • MAKES: 6½ DOZEN

2   cups sugar
1½ cups canola oil
2   large eggs
½   cup molasses
4   cups all-purpose flour
4   tsp. baking soda
3   tsp. ground ginger
2   tsp. ground cinnamon
1   tsp. salt
     Additional sugar
2   pkg. (10 to 12 oz. each)
     white baking chips
¼   cup shortening

1. Preheat oven to 350°. In a large bowl, combine sugar and oil. Beat in eggs. Stir in molasses. Combine the flour, baking soda, ginger, cinnamon and salt; gradually add to creamed mixture and mix well.

2. Shape into 1-in. balls and roll in sugar. Place 2 in. apart on ungreased baking sheets. Bake until cookies spring back when touched lightly, 10-12 minutes. Remove to wire racks to cool completely.

3. In a microwave, melt chips and shortening; stir until smooth. Dip cookies halfway into the melted chips or drizzle with mixture; allow excess to drip off. Place on waxed paper; let stand until set.

1 COOKIE: 105 cal., 5g fat (1g sat. fat), 5mg chol., 98mg sod., 14g carb. (9g sugars, 0 fiber), 1g pro.

FRESH FROM FROZEN
You can prepare the dough for these gingersnaps when time allows and bake at a later date. Roll the dough into balls and freeze in a single layer on a tray lined with parchment. Once frozen, transfer to freezer containers and freeze for up to 3 months. To bake frozen gingersnaps, roll in sugar and bake as directed, increasing the bake time by a few minutes if needed.

CHAPTER 4

Piped Cookies

Holiday Mocha Spritz

When I began to use my spritz press, this was the first flavor combination I tried.
It took a few attempts to get the hang of it, but now I'm playing with a new dough and
disk every time I make them. I plan on making several batches throughout the year.
—*Shelly Bevington, Hermiston, OR*

PREP: 35 MIN. • **BAKE:** 10 MIN./BATCH • **MAKES:** ABOUT 10 DOZEN

1½ **cups unsalted butter,
   softened**
1 **cup sugar**
1 **large egg, room
   temperature**
1 **Tbsp. instant coffee
   granules**
1 **tsp. vanilla extract**
3½ **cups all-purpose flour**
⅓ **cup dark baking cocoa
   or baking cocoa**
2 **tsp. instant espresso
   powder**
1 **tsp. baking powder**
½ **tsp. salt**
½ **tsp. ground nutmeg**
⅓ **cup orange juice
   Colored nonpareils,
   optional**

1. Preheat oven to 375°. In a large bowl, beat butter and sugar until light and fluffy, 5-7 minutes. Combine egg, instant coffee and vanilla; beat into creamed mixture. In another bowl, whisk flour, cocoa, espresso powder, baking powder, salt and nutmeg; add to the creamed mixture alternately with orange juice, beating well after each addition.

2. Using a cookie press fitted with a disk of your choice, press dough 1 in. apart onto ungreased baking sheets. If desired, sprinkle with nonpareils. Bake until set, 8-10 minutes (do not brown). Remove from pans to wire racks to cool.

1 COOKIE: 42 cal., 2g fat (1g sat. fat), 8mg chol., 15mg sod., 5g carb. (2g sugars, 0 fiber), 1g pro.

Italian Cornmeal Spritz Cookies

A chef at a local culinary school gave me this recipe, and I've been using it for years.
Italian cornmeal cookies are from the Piedmont region of northern Italy.
They're not too sweet, and the glazed cherries add just the right touch.
—*Kristine Chayes, Smithtown, NY*

PREP: 35 MIN. • **BAKE:** 10 MIN./BATCH • **MAKES:** 5½ DOZEN

1. Preheat oven to 325°. In a large bowl, cream butter and sugar until light and fluffy, 5-7 minutes. Beat in eggs and extracts. In another bowl, whisk flour and cornmeal; gradually beat into creamed mixture.

2. Using a cookie press fitted with a flower or star disk, press dough 1 in. apart onto ungreased baking sheets. Top each with a cherry piece.

3. Bake 9-11 minutes or until set. Remove from pans to wire racks to cool.

⅔ cup butter, softened
½ cup sugar
2 large eggs, room
   temperature
1 tsp. vanilla extract
½ tsp. almond extract
1¾ cups all-purpose flour
⅔ cup yellow cornmeal
   Red candied cherries,
   quartered

1 COOKIE: 47 cal., 2g fat (1g sat. fat), 11mg chol., 18mg sod., 6g carb. (2g sugars, 0 fiber), 1g pro.

Chocolate Meringue Stars

These light and delicate cookies are always a hit. Their big chocolate flavor makes it difficult to keep the kids away from them long enough to get any on the cookie tray!
—*Edna Lee, Greeley, CO*

PREP: 25 MIN. + STANDING • **BAKE:** 30 MIN./BATCH + COOLING • **MAKES:** ABOUT 4 DOZEN

3 **large egg whites**
¾ **tsp. vanilla extract**
¾ **cup sugar**
¼ **cup baking cocoa**

GLAZE
3 **oz. semisweet chocolate, chopped**
1 **Tbsp. shortening**

1. Place egg whites in a large bowl; let stand at room temperature for 30 minutes.

2. Add vanilla to egg whites; beat on medium speed until soft peaks form. Gradually add sugar, about 2 Tbsp. at a time, beating until stiff peaks form and sugar is dissolved. Gently fold in cocoa.

3. Line baking sheets with parchment. Insert a large open star tip into a pastry bag; fill half full with meringue. Pipe stars (about 1¼-in. diameter) onto prepared sheets, or drop by rounded teaspoonfuls .

4. Bake until lightly browned, 30-35 minutes. Remove from pans; cool completely on wire racks.

5. In a microwave, melt chocolate and shortening; stir until smooth. Dip cookies halfway into glaze; allow excess to drip off. Place on waxed paper; let stand until set.

1 MERINGUE: 27 cal., 1g fat (0 sat. fat), 0 chol., 3mg sod., 4g carb. (3g sugars, 0 fiber), 0 pro.

Pistachio Meringue Sandwich Cookies

Traditional macarons are confections made with egg whites, sugar and almonds. Our easy version calls for pistachios and features a rich chocolate filling.
—Taste of Home *Test Kitchen*

PREP: 35 MIN. + COOLING • **BAKE:** 10 MIN./BATCH + COOLING • **MAKES:** ABOUT 1½ DOZEN

3 **large egg whites**
1¼ **cups confectioners' sugar**
¾ **cup pistachios**
   Dash salt
¼ **cup sugar**
   Green paste food coloring, optional

CHOCOLATE FILLING
4 **oz. bittersweet chocolate, chopped**
½ **cup heavy whipping cream**
2 **tsp. corn syrup**
1 **Tbsp. butter**

1. Let egg whites stand at room temperature for 30 minutes. Pulse confectioners' sugar and pistachios in a food processor until powdery.

2. Preheat oven to 350°. Add salt to the egg whites; beat on medium speed until soft peaks form. Gradually add sugar, 1 Tbsp. at a time, beating on high until stiff peaks form. Fold in pistachio mixture and, if desired, green food coloring.

3. Transfer pistachio mixture to a pastry bag fitted with a round tip. Pipe 1-in.-diameter cookies 1 in. apart onto parchment-lined baking sheets. Bake until lightly browned and firm to the touch, 10-12 minutes. Cool completely on pans on wire racks.

4. Place chocolate in a small bowl. In a small saucepan, bring cream and corn syrup just to a boil. Pour over chocolate; whisk until smooth. Whisk in butter. Cool, stirring occasionally, to room temperature or until filling reaches a spreading consistency, about 45 minutes. Spread on the bottoms of half the cookies; cover with remaining cookies. If desired, roll edges in additional chopped pistachios.

1 SANDWICH COOKIE: 160 cal., 9g fat (4g sat. fat), 10mg chol., 135mg sod., 16g carb. (14g sugars, 1g fiber), 3g pro.

Hazelnut Macarons

You don't have to be an expert in French cooking to create these sandwich cookies. The crisp, chewy macarons require attention to detail, but they're not hard to make— and they're simply a delight, both for personal snacking and giving as gifts!
—Taste of Home *Test Kitchen*

PREP: 50 MIN. + COOLING • BAKE: 10 MIN./BATCH + COOLING • MAKES: ABOUT 5 DOZEN

6 **large egg whites**
1½ **cups hazelnuts, toasted**
2½ **cups confectioners'**
 sugar
 Dash salt
½ **cup superfine sugar**

COFFEE BUTTERCREAM
1 **cup sugar**
6 **Tbsp. water**
6 **large egg yolks**
4 **tsp. instant espresso**
 powder
1 **tsp. vanilla extract**
1½ **cups butter, softened**
6 **Tbsp. confectioners'**
 sugar

1. Place egg whites in a small bowl; let stand at room temperature for 30 minutes.

2. Preheat the oven to 350°. Place hazelnuts and confectioners' sugar in a food processor; pulse until nuts are finely ground.

3. Add salt to egg whites; beat on medium speed until soft peaks form. Gradually add superfine sugar, 1 Tbsp. at a time, beating on high until stiff peaks form. Fold in the hazelnut mixture.

4. Transfer mixture to a pastry bag fitted with a round tip. Pipe 1-in.-diameter cookies 2 in. apart onto parchment-lined baking sheets. Bake until lightly browned and firm to the touch, 9-12 minutes. Transfer cookies on the parchment to wire racks; cool completely.

5. For the buttercream, in a heavy saucepan, combine sugar and water. Bring to a boil; cook over medium-high heat until sugar is dissolved. Remove from heat. In a small bowl, whisk a small amount of hot syrup into the egg yolks; return all to pan, whisking constantly. Cook until thickened, 2-3 minutes, stirring constantly; remove from the heat. Stir in the espresso powder and vanilla; cool completely.

6. In a stand mixer with the whisk attachment, beat butter until creamy. Gradually beat in cooled syrup. Beat in confectioners' sugar until fluffy. Refrigerate until mixture firms to a spreading consistency, about 10 minutes.

7. Spread about 1½ tsp buttercream onto the bottoms of half the cookies; top with remaining cookies. Store in airtight containers in the refrigerator.

NOTE: To toast whole hazelnuts, bake in a shallow pan in a 350° oven until fragrant and lightly browned, 7-10 minutes, stirring occasionally. To remove skins, wrap hazelnuts in a tea towel; rub with towel to loosen skins.

1 SANDWICH COOKIE: 117 cal., 8g fat (3g sat. fat), 31mg chol., 67mg sod., 12g carb. (11g sugars, 0 fiber), 1g pro.

Mint Twist Meringues

Meringues flavored with peppermint are a yuletide tradition, but I also use extracts like almond and vanilla to make these crispy delights year-round.
—*Cheryl Perry, Hertford, NC*

PREP: 30 MIN. • BAKE: 40 MIN. + COOLING • MAKES: 2 DOZEN

2 **large egg whites**
½ **tsp. cream of tartar**
¼ **tsp. peppermint extract**
½ **cup sugar**
¼ **cup crushed red mint candies**

1. Place egg whites in a small bowl; let stand at room temperature for 30 minutes.

2. Preheat oven to 250°. Add cream of tartar and extract to egg whites; beat on medium speed until foamy. Gradually add sugar, 1 Tbsp. at a time, beating on high after each addition until sugar is dissolved. Continue beating until stiff glossy peaks form.

3. Transfer meringue to a pastry bag fitted with a plain piping tip. Pipe 1½-in.-diameter cookies 2 in. apart onto parchment-lined baking sheets. Sprinkle with crushed candies.

4. Bake until firm to the touch, 40-45 minutes. Turn oven off; leave meringues in oven 1 hour. Remove from pans to a wire rack. Store in an airtight container.

1 COOKIE: 17 cal., 0 fat (0 sat. fat), 0 chol., 5mg sod., 4g carb. (3g sugars, 0 fiber), 0 pro.

READER REVIEW
"These were wonderful! So simple and easy to make!"
—SANDRAMCLURE, TASTEOFHOME.COM

Buttery Spritz Cookies

This tender spritz cookie recipe is quite eye-catching on my Christmas cookie tray. The dough is easy to work with, so it's fun to make these into a variety of festive shapes.
—*Beverly Launius, Sandwich, IL*

PREP: 20 MIN. • BAKE: 10 MIN./BATCH + COOLING • MAKES: ABOUT 7½ DOZEN

1 cup butter, softened
2¼ cups confectioners' sugar, divided
½ tsp. salt
1 large egg, room temperature
1 tsp. vanilla extract
½ tsp. almond extract
2½ cups all-purpose flour
2 to 3 Tbsp. water
Colored sugar and sprinkles
Melted semisweet chocolate or melted chocolate candy coating, optional

1. Preheat oven to 375°. In a large bowl, cream butter, 1¼ cups confectioners' sugar and salt until light and fluffy, 5-7 minutes. Beat in egg and extracts. Gradually beat flour into creamed mixture.

2. Using a cookie press fitted with a disk of your choice, press dough 2 in. apart onto ungreased baking sheets. Bake until set, 6-8 minutes (do not brown). Remove to wire racks to cool completely.

3. In a small bowl, mix the remaining 1 cup confectioners' sugar and enough water to reach desired consistency. Dip cookies into glaze; sprinkle with colored sugar and sprinkles. Let stand until set. Or, if desired, dip in melted chocolate, decorate and let stand until set.

1 COOKIE: 43 cal., 2g fat (1g sat. fat), 7mg chol., 30mg sod., 6g carb. (3g sugars, 0 fiber), 0 pro.

NO PRESS-URE SPRITZ
If you don't have a cookie press, use a heavy-duty piping bag with different tips. Otherwise, you can use a cookie scoop to scoop the dough into 1-in. balls. Then, place on cookie sheets and press in a design with a fork, or flatten the balls slightly with your fingertips or with the bottom of a glass dipped in sugar. Bake as directed.

Lemon Cooler Cookies

Baking soda helps brown these crisp, lemony, shortbread-like goodies
created by our Test Kitchen experts. If you're a fan of lemon, you're sure to love these.
—Taste of Home *Test Kitchen*

TAKES: 30 MIN. • **MAKES:** 3½ DOZEN

1. Preheat oven to 350°. In a large bowl, beat the butter, oil and sugar. Beat in the egg, egg white, lemonade concentrate and lemon zest. Combine the flour, baking powder, salt and baking soda; gradually add to the egg mixture.

2. Using a cookie press fitted with the disk of your choice, press dough 2 in. apart onto ungreased baking sheets. Sprinkle with yellow sugar. Bake until edges are lightly browned, 8-10 minutes. Cool on wire racks.

1 COOKIE: 58 cal., 2g fat (1g sat. fat), 7mg chol., 36mg sod., 9g carb. (5g sugars, 0 fiber), 1g pro.

¼ cup butter, softened
2 Tbsp. canola oil
¾ cup sugar
1 large egg, room
   temperature
1 large egg white, room
   temperature
¼ cup thawed lemonade
   concentrate
2 tsp. grated lemon zest
2 cups all-purpose flour
½ tsp. baking powder
¼ tsp. salt
⅛ tsp. baking soda
1 Tbsp. yellow decorating
   sugar

LOTSA LEMON—OR NONE AT ALL
For an extra punch of lemon flavor, whisk in a little powdered lemonade mix with the sugar coating.
If you don't love lemon, try substituting orange juice or limeade concentrate and zest for the lemon.

Vanilla Meringue Cookies

These sweet little swirls are light as can be. They're all you need after a big, special dinner.
—*Jenni Sharp, Milwaukee, WI*

PREP: 20 MIN. • BAKE: 40 MIN. + COOLING • MAKES: ABOUT 5 DOZEN

3 **large egg whites**
1½ **tsp. clear or regular vanilla extract**
¼ **tsp. cream of tartar**
Dash salt
⅔ **cup sugar**

1. Place egg whites in a small bowl; let stand at room temperature 30 minutes.

2. Preheat oven to 250°. Add vanilla, cream of tartar and salt to egg whites; beat on medium speed until foamy. Gradually add sugar, 1 Tbsp. at a time, beating on high after each addition, until sugar is dissolved. Continue beating until stiff glossy peaks form, about 7 minutes.

3. Attach a #32 star tip to a pastry bag. Transfer meringue to bag. Pipe 1¼-in.-diameter cookies 2 in. apart onto parchment-lined baking sheets.

4. Bake until firm to the touch, 40-45 minutes. Turn off oven; leave meringues in oven 1 hour (leave oven door closed). Remove from oven; cool completely on baking sheets. Remove meringues from paper; store in an airtight container at room temperature.

1 COOKIE: 10 cal., 0 fat (0 sat. fat), 0 chol., 5mg sod., 2g carb. (2g sugars, 0 fiber), 0 pro. **DIABETIC EXCHANGES:** 1 free food.

MERINGUE MISSTEPS
If your meringues are flat, it's usually because of lack of air. Be sure to follow the instructions for beating. Starting slowly will make foam, which means bubbles of air. Adding the sugar all at once will weigh down the whites and break the bubbles.

If the meringues are chewy, it's probably because they weren't baked long enough. Check the bake time and make sure cookies stay in the oven according to the recipe directions (no peeking!).

Holiday Meringue Miniatures

My kids love these light, melt-in-your-mouth cookies,
and we have fun making them. These were always on our
Christmas cookie plate when I was a kid, and now the tradition continues.
—*Susan Marshall, Colorado Springs, CO*

PREP: 20 MIN. • **BAKE:** 1 HOUR + COOLING • **MAKES:** ABOUT 7 DOZEN

2 large egg whites,
room temperature
½ tsp. white vinegar
Dash salt
½ tsp. almond extract
½ tsp. vanilla extract
½ cup sugar
Red gel food coloring

1. Preheat oven to 225°. Beat egg whites with vinegar and salt on medium speed until foamy and doubled in volume. Beat in extracts. Gradually add sugar, 1 Tbsp. at a time, beating on high after each addition until sugar is dissolved. Continue beating until stiff glossy peaks form, about 10 minutes.

2. Insert a ½-in. round tip into a pastry bag. Paint 5 stripes of red food coloring inside the length of the pastry bag. Transfer meringue to pastry bag; pipe dollops 1 in. apart onto parchment-lined baking sheets.

3. Bake 1 hour or until set and dry. Turn off oven (do not open oven door); leave meringues in oven for 1 hour. Remove and cool completely on baking sheets. Remove meringues from paper; store in an airtight container at room temperature.

1 MERINGUE: 5 cal., 0 fat (0 sat. fat), 0 chol., 19mg sod., 1g carb. (1g sugars, 0 fiber), 0 pro. **DIABETIC EXCHANGES:** 1 free food.

DO THE PEPPERMINT TWIST
Feel free to mix up the extracts and food coloring—using peppermint extract to match the red stripes, or spearmint extract and green stripes. These little meringues would also make a stunning cake topper.

Maple-Walnut Spritz Cookies

After taking a trip to Vermont during maple harvest season and tasting some amazing maple goodies, I just had to make something using maple syrup. The answer was this delicious cookie. I love walnuts, maple syrup and spritz cookies, so I used all those elements to create these perfectly scrumptious bites.
—*Paula Marchesi, Lenhartsville, PA*

PREP: 30 MIN. • BAKE: 10 MIN./BATCH • MAKES: 6½ DOZEN

1. Preheat oven to 350°. In a bowl, cream butter and brown sugar until light and fluffy, 3-4 minutes. Beat in egg, maple syrup and vanilla. In another bowl, whisk flour, ground walnuts, baking powder and salt; gradually beat into the creamed mixture (dough will be soft).

2. Using a cookie press fitted with a flower or star disk, press dough 1 in. apart onto ungreased baking sheets. Sprinkle with coarse sugar. Top with walnuts.

3. Bake until bottoms are light brown, 10-12 minutes. Cool on pans 2 minutes. Remove to wire racks to cool.

1 COOKIE: 38 cal., 2g fat (1g sat. fat), 6mg chol., 21mg sod., 4g carb. (2g sugars, 0 fiber), 1g pro.

½ cup butter, softened
⅓ cup packed brown sugar
1 large egg, room temperature
¼ cup maple syrup
1 tsp. vanilla extract
1½ cups all-purpose flour
⅔ cup ground walnuts
½ tsp. baking powder
¼ tsp. salt
Coarse sugar
⅔ cup walnut pieces

READER REVIEW
"The perfect light, crispy, nutty, not-too-sweet cookie. It was my first attempt at the cookie press, so some were prettier than others, but all were still delicious."
—KENDRA608, TASTEOFHOME.COM

Chocolate Chip Meringue Cookies

This is one of my most popular recipes. I usually make them as round cookies, but for Valentine's Day I will pipe them into heart shapes.
—*Debbie Tilley, Riverview, FL*

PREP: 20 MIN. • BAKE: 20 MIN. + COOLING • MAKES: 2 DOZEN

3 **large egg whites, room temperature**
¼ **tsp. cream of tartar**
¼ **tsp. salt**
1 **cup sugar**
3 **Tbsp. baking cocoa**
3 **Tbsp. miniature semisweet chocolate chips**
3 **Tbsp. finely crushed almonds or walnuts, optional**

1. Preheat oven to 300°. In a large bowl, beat egg whites until foamy. Add cream of tartar and salt; beat until soft peaks form. Gradually add sugar, 1 Tbsp. at a time, beating on high speed until stiff peaks form, about 6 minutes. Beat in cocoa. Fold in chocolate chips and, if desired, nuts.

2. Transfer meringue mixture to a pastry bag fitted with a round tip. Pipe 1-in.-diameter cookies 1 in. apart onto parchment-lined baking sheets.

3. Bake until firm to the touch, 20-25 minutes. Turn off oven (do not open oven door); leave meringues in oven 1 hour. Remove and cool completely on baking sheets. Remove meringues from paper; store in an airtight container at room temperature.

1 COOKIE: 43 cal., 0 fat (0 sat. fat), 0 chol., 32mg sod., 10g carb. (9g sugars, 0 fiber), 1g pro.

READER REVIEW
"Spectacular! It is hard to imagine the deep, rich flavor of such a light cookie. I followed the directions except I dropped the cookies instead of piping them. They still turned out beautiful. I also included ½ teaspoon vanilla. This is great to make on the same day as making a pound cake that uses only egg yolks."
—MAMAKNOWSBEST, TASTEOFHOME.COM

Cranberry Spritz Cookies

Here's a sure standout on your treat tray. The cheery cookies get their bright pink color from cranberry-flavored gelatin.
—*Kristen Rahn, Burnsville, MN*

PREP: 30 MIN. • **BAKE:** 10 MIN./BATCH + COOLING • **MAKES:** 5 DOZEN

1. Preheat oven to 375°. In a large bowl, cream butter, shortening, sugar and gelatin until light and fluffy, 5-7 minutes. Beat in egg and vanilla. Combine flour, baking powder and salt; gradually add to the creamed mixture and mix well.

2. Using a cookie press fitted with the disk of your choice, press dough 2 in. apart onto ungreased baking sheets. If desired, sprinkle with coarse sugar.

3. Bake until set (do not brown), 6-8 minutes. Remove to wire racks to cool completely.

½ cup butter, softened
½ cup butter-flavored shortening
½ cup sugar
¼ cup cranberry gelatin powder (about 4 oz.)
1 large egg, room temperature
1 tsp. vanilla extract
2 cups all-purpose flour
½ tsp. baking powder
¼ tsp. salt
Colored coarse sugar, optional

1 COOKIE: 58 cal., 3g fat (1g sat. fat), 8mg chol., 27mg sod., 6g carb. (3g sugars, 0 fiber), 1g pro.

Chocolate-Topped Peanut Butter Spritz

Peanut butter gives these delicious cookies a different flavor
from other spritz. The chocolate drizzle makes them extra special.
—*Dolores Deegan, Pottstown, PA*

PREP: 25 MIN. + CHILLING • **BAKE:** 10 MIN./BATCH + COOLING • **MAKES:** 16 DOZEN

1. Preheat oven to 350°. In a large bowl, cream butter, peanut butter and sugars. Add eggs, 1 at a time, beating well after each addition. Combine flour, soda and salt; gradually add to the creamed mixture. Chill 15 minutes.

2. Using a cookie press fitted with bar disk, form dough into long strips on ungreased baking sheets. Cut each strip into 2-in. pieces (there is no need to separate the pieces). Bake for 6-8 minutes. (Watch carefully—cookies brown quickly.)

3. For topping, melt chocolate with shortening; stir until blended. Place in a heavy plastic bag; cut a small hole in the corner. Pipe a strip of chocolate down center of each cookie; sprinkle with chopped peanuts.

1 COOKIE: 37 cal., 2g fat (1g sat. fat), 4mg chol., 27mg sod., 4g carb. (3g sugars, 0 fiber), 1g pro.

1 **cup butter, softened**
1 **cup peanut butter**
1 **cup sugar**
1 **cup packed brown sugar**
2 **large eggs, room temperature**
2 **cups all-purpose flour**
1 **tsp. baking soda**
½ **tsp. salt**

CHOCOLATE TOPPING
1½ **cups semisweet chocolate chips**
1 **Tbsp. shortening**
 Chopped peanuts

Sparkly Meringue Snowmen

For my son's first Christmas home from Iraq, I wanted everything to feel magical.
He loves meringue cookies, so I made a big batch of minty snowflakes and snowmen.
—*Patricia Lindsay, Independence, KS*

PREP: 30 MIN. • BAKE: 80 MIN. + COOLING • MAKES: ABOUT 1 DOZEN

2 **large egg whites**
⅛ **tsp. cream of tartar**
½ **cup sugar**
½ **tsp. mint or vanilla**
    extract
    Black nonpareils
    Orange sprinkles

1. Place egg whites in a large bowl; let stand at room temperature 30 minutes.

2. Preheat oven to 200°. Add cream of tartar to egg whites; beat on medium speed until foamy. Gradually add sugar, 1 Tbsp. at a time, beating on high after each addition until sugar is dissolved. Continue beating until stiff glossy peaks form. Fold in extract.

3. Transfer meringue to a pastry bag fitted with a #12 round tip. Pipe snowmen about 4 in. tall, 2 in. apart, onto parchment-lined baking sheets. Decorate with black nonpareils and orange sprinkles. Bake until firm to the touch, 80-90 minutes.

4. Remove to wire racks to cool completely. Store in an airtight container.

1 COOKIE: 31 cal., 0 fat (0 sat. fat), 0 chol., 8mg sod., 7g carb. (7g sugars, 0 fiber), 1g pro. **DIABETIC EXCHANGES:** ½ starch.

Festive Meringue Cookies

These festive treats sparkle not only during the holidays but for other occasions year-round. Use colored sugar or food coloring to change things up.
—Taste of Home *Test Kitchen*

PREP: 15 MIN. • **BAKE:** 35 MIN. + COOLING • **MAKES:** ABOUT 2 DOZEN

3 **large egg whites, room temperature**
½ **tsp. vanilla extract**
¾ **cup sugar**
White pearl or coarse sugar, optional

1. Preheat oven to 250°. Beat egg whites on medium speed until foamy; add vanilla. Beat until soft peaks form. Gradually beat in sugar, 1 Tbsp. at a time, beating on high after each addition until sugar is dissolved. Continue beating until stiff glossy peaks form.

2. Transfer meringue to a pastry bag fitted with a large star tip. Pipe 2-in. circles or shapes 2 in. apart onto parchment-lined baking sheets. If desired, sprinkle with pearl or coarse sugar.

3. Bake until set and dry, 35-40 minutes. Turn oven off (do not open oven door); leave meringues in oven for 1½ hours. Remove from oven; cool completely on baking sheets. Store in an airtight container at room temperature.

1 MERINGUE: 27 cal., 0 fat (0 sat. fat), 0 chol., 7mg sod., 6g carb. (6g sugars, 0 fiber), 0 pro. **DIABETIC EXCHANGES:** ½ starch.

Mocha Meringue Sandwich Cookies

These crisp, chewy cookies can be made any size you choose. They're also outstanding with a variety of fillings—try making them with fruit preserves.
—Marie Valdes, Brandon, FL

PREP: 30 MIN. • **BAKE:** 15 MIN./BATCH + COOLING • **MAKES:** ABOUT 2 DOZEN

1. Preheat oven to 350°. Place egg whites in a large bowl. In a small bowl, sift coffee granules through a fine sieve to break up, pressing with a spoon as needed. Sift together ½ cup confectioners' sugar, cocoa and coffee.

2. Add cream of tartar to egg whites; beat on medium speed until foamy. Gradually beat in sugar, 1 Tbsp. at a time, beating on high after each addition until sugar is dissolved. Continue beating until stiff glossy peaks form. Fold in coffee mixture.

3. Transfer the meringue to a pastry bag fitted with a #11 round pastry tip; pipe 1¾-in. spirals 1 in. apart onto parchment-lined baking sheets.

4. Bake meringues until set and dry, 12-15 minutes. Cool completely before removing meringues from paper.

5. To assemble, spread about 1½ tsp. frosting onto the bottom of half of the meringues; cover with remaining meringues. Dust with additional confectioners' sugar.

- **3 large egg whites, room temperature**
- **1 tsp. instant coffee granules**
- **½ cup confectioners' sugar**
- **¼ cup baking cocoa**
- **¼ tsp. cream of tartar**
- **¾ cup sugar**
- **¾ cup chocolate frosting Additional confectioners' sugar**

1 SANDWICH COOKIE: 76 cal., 2g fat (1g sat. fat), 0 chol., 25mg sod., 15g carb. (14g sugars, 0 fiber), 1g pro.
DIABETIC EXCHANGES: 1 starch, ½ fat.

Grandma's Spritz Cookies

I use my grandmother's antique cookie press to make these festive cookies.
I'm the only one in the family who can still get it to work!
—*Suzanne Kern, Louisville, KY*

PREP: 15 MIN. • BAKE: 10 MIN./BATCH • MAKES: 6½ DOZEN

1 cup shortening
¾ cup sugar
1 large egg, room
    temperature
1 tsp. almond extract
2¼ cups all-purpose flour
½ tsp. baking powder
    Dash salt
    Optional: Assorted
    sprinkles and
    colored sugar

1. Preheat oven to 400°. In a large mixing bowl, cream shortening and sugar until light and fluffy, 5-7 minutes. Add egg and almond extract; mix well. Combine flour, baking powder and salt; add to the creamed mixture until blended.

2. Using a cookie press fitted with the disk of your choice, press dough shapes 2 in. apart onto ungreased baking sheets. If desired, sprinkle with toppings. Bake until set (do not brown), 7-8 minutes.

1 COOKIE: 44 cal., 3g fat (1g sat. fat), 2mg chol., 6mg sod., 5g carb. (2g sugars, 0 fiber), 0 pro.

STOP THE SPREAD!
If your spritz cookies are spreading, there are a few tricks you can try. First, make sure you're using ungreased, unlined cookie sheets, because classic spritz cookies require ungreased metal to grip (and won't stick when baking). You can also try chilling the dough, but make sure to keep an eye on it—the dough needs to be pliable enough to go through the press. A chilled baking sheet can also help.

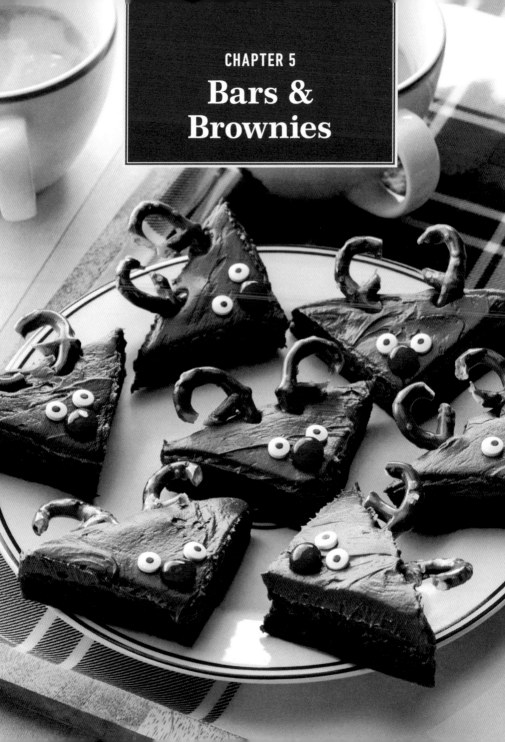

Reindeer Brownies

My grown son, Jeremy, acts as if he's 5 when he sees these brownies—
I've been making them for more than 30 years. My daughter, Jayme, and my four
grandchildren love them too. If you're short on time, a boxed mix works just fine.
—*Jeannine Schneider, Fremont, CA*

PREP: 30 MIN. • BAKE: 25 MIN. + COOLING • MAKES: 2 DOZEN

4 oz. unsweetened chocolate, chopped
¾ cup butter, cubed
3 large eggs, room temperature
2 cups sugar
1 tsp. vanilla extract
¼ tsp. salt
1 cup all-purpose flour
1 can (16 oz.) chocolate frosting
48 candy eyeballs
24 red-hot candies
48 miniature pretzels

1. Preheat oven to 350°. Line a 13x9-in. baking pan with foil, letting the ends extend up the sides; grease foil. In a microwave, melt chocolate and butter; stir until smooth. Cool slightly.

2. Whisk eggs, sugar, vanilla and salt until blended; stir in chocolate mixture. Gradually stir in flour; spread into prepared pan. Bake until edges begin to pull from sides of pan, 25-30 minutes. Cool completely in pan on a wire rack.

3. Lifting with the foil, remove the brownies from pan. Spread frosting over top. Cut into 12 squares; cut each square into 2 triangles. Attach candies and pretzels to make reindeer faces.

1 BROWNIE: 353 cal., 16g fat (8g sat. fat), 51mg chol., 243mg sod., 50g carb. (37g sugars, 1g fiber), 3g pro.

Frosted Apricot Almond Bars

I often bring these treats to Christmas potlucks and parties.
A tin of these yummy bars makes a welcome gift.
—*Lynne Danley, Hillsboro, OR*

PREP: 20 MIN. • **BAKE:** 20 MIN. + COOLING • **MAKES:** 5 DOZEN

1 cup butter, softened
1 cup packed
   light brown sugar
½ tsp. salt
3 tsp. vanilla extract
3 cups all-purpose flour
1 jar (12 oz.) apricot
   preserves, warmed

ALMOND LAYER
2 cans (8 oz. each)
   almond paste,
   crumbled into small
   pieces
1 cup sugar
2 tsp. vanilla extract
4 large eggs

FROSTING
2 oz. unsweetened
   chocolate, chopped
½ cup half-and-half
   cream
3 cups confectioners'
   sugar
¼ cup butter, softened
2 tsp. vanilla extract

1. Preheat oven to 350°. Cream butter, brown sugar and salt until light and fluffy, 5-7 minutes. Beat in vanilla. Gradually beat in flour. Press onto bottom of a greased 15x10x1-in. baking pan. Spread with preserves.

2. In another bowl, beat almond paste and sugar on low speed until blended. Beat in vanilla and eggs, 1 at a time. Pour over preserves.

3. Bake for 20-25 minutes or until a toothpick inserted in almond layer comes out clean. Cool slightly on a wire rack.

4. Meanwhile, place chocolate in a large bowl. In a small saucepan, bring cream just to a boil; pour over chocolate. Stir with a whisk until smooth. Add confectioners' sugar, butter and vanilla; beat until smooth. Spread over warm bars. Cool completely before cutting.

1 BAR: 170 cal., 7g fat (3g sat. fat), 24mg chol., 60mg sod., 25g carb. (18g sugars, 1g fiber), 2g pro.

Macaroon Bars

Guests will never recognize the refrigerated crescent roll dough that goes into these almond-flavored bars. You can assemble the chewy coconut treats in no time.
—*Carolyn Kyzer, Alexander, AR*

PREP: 10 MIN. • BAKE: 30 MIN. + COOLING • MAKES: 3 DOZEN

1. Preheat oven to 350°. Grease a 13x9-in. baking pan; line pan with nonstick foil, allowing the foil to hang over edges of pan. Grease the foil; sprinkle 1½ cups coconut into pan. Combine milk and extract; drizzle half over the coconut. Unroll crescent dough into 1 long rectangle; seal seams and perforations. Place in pan. Drizzle with the remaining milk mixture; sprinkle with remaining coconut.

2. Bake for 30-35 minutes or until golden brown. Cool completely on a wire rack before cutting into bars. Store in the refrigerator.

3¼ cups sweetened shredded coconut, divided
1 can (14 oz.) sweetened condensed milk
1 tsp. almond extract
1 tube (8 oz.) refrigerated crescent rolls

1 BAR: 103 cal., 5g fat (4g sat. fat), 4mg chol., 85mg sod., 12g carb. (9g sugars, 0 fiber), 2g protein.

READER REVIEW
"This recipe couldn't be simpler. I sprinkled thin almond slices on top before baking. It looked and tasted delicious!"
—MRS. COWAN, TASTEOFHOME.COM

Chocolate Caramel Bars

Taking dessert or another treat to a church or school potluck is never a problem for me. I jump at the chance to offer these rich, chocolaty bars.

—Steve Mirro, Cape Coral, FL

PREP: 15 MIN. • BAKE: 25 MIN. + COOLING • MAKES: 3 DOZEN

1 pkg. (11 oz.) caramels
1 can (5 oz.) evaporated milk, divided
¾ cup butter, softened
1 pkg. German chocolate cake mix (regular size)
2 cups semisweet chocolate chips

1. Pln a small saucepan over low heat, melt caramels with ¼ cup milk; stir until smooth. Meanwhile, in a large bowl, cream butter until light and fluffy, 5-7 minutes. Beat in dry cake mix and remaining milk.

2. Spread half the dough into a greased 13x9-in. baking pan. Bake at 350° for 6 minutes; sprinkle with the chocolate chips.

3. Gently spread the caramel mixture over chips. Drop remaining dough by tablespoonfuls over the caramel layer. Return to oven for 15 minutes. Cool completely; cut into bars.

1 BAR: 185 cal., 9g fat (5g sat. fat), 12mg chol., 161mg sod., 26g carb. (19g sugars, 1g fiber), 2g pro.

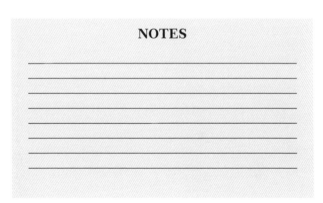

NOTES

Maple Butterscotch Brownies

I often make a double batch of these brownies—they go fast no matter where I take them! I've baked them for family dinners and church suppers, and I always come back with an empty pan. They are easy to make and freeze well.
—*Grace Vonhold, Rochester, NY*

PREP: 15 MIN. • **BAKE:** 30 MIN. + COOLING • **MAKES:** 16 BROWNIES

1. Preheat oven to 350°. Whisk together the flour and baking powder.

2. In a large bowl, mix brown sugar, melted butter and maple flavoring. Beat in eggs, 1 at a time, mixing well after each addition. Stir in flour mixture and walnuts. Spread into a greased 9-in. square baking pan.

3. Bake until a toothpick inserted in the center comes out clean, 27-32 minutes. Cool completely in pan on a wire rack. If desired, dust with confectioners' sugar. Cut into bars.

1 BROWNIE: 216 cal., 11g fat (4g sat. fat), 42mg chol., 98mg sod., 27g carb. (17g sugars, 1g fiber), 4g pro.

1½ cups all-purpose flour
1 tsp. baking powder
1¼ cups packed brown sugar
½ cup butter, melted
1½ tsp. maple flavoring
2 large eggs, room temperature
1 cup chopped walnuts
Confectioners' sugar, optional

Chocolate Oat Squares

When you bring these chewy treats to a group meal, guests will be tempted to start at the dessert table. Chock-full of chocolate and walnuts, they'll satisfy any sweet tooth.

—Jennifer Eilts, Lincoln, NE

PREP: 20 MIN. • **BAKE:** 20 MIN. + COOLING • **MAKES:** 4 DOZEN

1 cup plus 2 Tbsp. butter, softened, divided
2 cups packed brown sugar
2 large eggs, room temperature
4 tsp. vanilla extract, divided
3 cups quick-cooking oats
2½ cups all-purpose flour
1½ tsp. salt, divided
1 tsp. baking soda
1 can (14 oz.) sweetened condensed milk
2 cups semisweet chocolate chips
1 cup chopped walnuts

1. Preheat oven to 350°. In a large bowl, beat 1 cup butter and the brown sugar until light and fluffy, 5-7 minutes. Beat in the eggs and 2 tsp. vanilla. Combine oats, flour, 1 tsp. salt and the baking soda; gradually add to creamed mixture and mix well. Press two-thirds of oat mixture into a greased 15x10x1-in. baking pan.

2. In a large saucepan, combine milk, chocolate chips, remaining 2 Tbsp. butter and remaining ½ tsp. salt. Cook and stir over low heat until chocolate is melted. Remove from the heat; stir in walnuts and the remaining 2 tsp. vanilla. Spread over crust. Sprinkle with remaining oat mixture.

3. Bake until golden brown, 20-25 minutes. Cool completely in pan on a wire rack. Cut into squares.

1 SQUARE: 205 cal., 10g fat (5g sat. fat), 23mg chol., 155mg sod., 28g carb. (19g sugars, 1g fiber), 3g pro.

Candy Cane Shortbread Bars

I created these bars for my daughter, who loves peppermint. The delicate, buttery shortbread melts in your mouth. They're a hit wherever I take them.
—*Susan Ciuffreda, Huntersville, NC*

PREP: 30 MIN. • BAKE: 20 MIN. + COOLING • MAKES: 2 DOZEN

1 cup butter, softened
1 cup packed
  brown sugar
1 large egg yolk,
  room temperature
1½ tsp. peppermint extract
2 cups all-purpose flour

BUTTERCREAM
2 cups confectioners'
  sugar
¼ cup butter, melted
2 Tbsp. 2% milk
½ tsp. peppermint extract
2 drops red food
  coloring, optional

TOPPING
9 oz. white baking
  chocolate, melted
  and cooled slightly
¾ cup crushed candy
  canes (about 10 regular)

1. Preheat oven to 350°. Line a 13x9-in. baking pan with parchment, letting ends extend up sides.

2. In a large bowl, cream butter and brown sugar until light and fluffy, 5-7 minutes. Beat in the egg yolk and extract. Gradually beat in flour. Press evenly into prepared pan.

3. Bake for 16-19 minutes or until edges are brown. Cool completely in pan on a wire rack.

4. In a bowl, combine buttercream ingredients; beat until smooth. Spread over shortbread. Carefully spread the melted white chocolate over top. Sprinkle with candy canes; let stand until set.

5. Lifting with parchment, remove shortbread from pan. Cut into bars.

1 BAR: 265 cal., 13g fat (8g sat. fat), 33mg chol., 97mg sod., 37g carb. (27g sugars, 0 fiber), 2g pro.

Caramel-Pecan Cookie Butter Bars

One day I was thinking about a way to use cookie butter and came up with this recipe. They were an instant hit in my house. These bars freeze well—they are so tempting to remove from the freezer one by one until there are no more left.

—Sheryl Little, Cabot, AR

PREP: 15 MIN. • BAKE: 15 MIN. + COOLING • MAKES: 2 DOZEN

1. Preheat oven to 375°. In a large bowl, cream the butter, sugars and cookie butter until light and fluffy, 5-7 minutes. Beat in egg. Gradually beat in the flour. Spread onto the bottom of a greased 13x9-in. baking pan. Sprinkle with pecans; press lightly into dough. Bake until edges are lightly browned, 15-20 minutes.

2. Meanwhile, in a large saucepan, combine the caramels and cream. Cook and stir over medium-low heat until caramels are melted. Remove from heat; stir in vanilla. Pour over crust. Cool completely in pan on a wire rack.

- ½ **cup butter, softened**
- ½ **cup sugar**
- ½ **cup packed brown sugar**
- ½ **cup Biscoff creamy cookie spread**
- 1 **large egg, room temperature**
- 1¼ **cups self-rising flour**
- 2 **cups pecan halves, coarsely chopped**
- 1 **pkg. (11 oz.) caramels**
- 3 **Tbsp. half-and-half cream**
- 1 **tsp. vanilla extract**
- 1 **cup (6 oz.) dark chocolate chips**
- 1 **Tbsp. shortening**

3. In a microwave, melt chocolate chips and shortening; stir until smooth. Drizzle over top; let stand until set. Cut into bars.

1 BAR: 285 cal., 17g fat (6g sat. fat), 20mg chol., 149mg sod., 34g carb. (25g sugars, 2g fiber), 3g pro.

Baileys & Mint Brownie Cheesecake Bites

This is a combo of two St. Patrick's Day goodies, but I make the bars year round. You can use any type of chips in the brownies, and you can choose to swirl in the cheesecake instead of using it as a separate topping.

—Teri Rasey, Cadillac, MI

PREP: 25 MIN. • **BAKE:** 45 MIN. + CHILLING • **MAKES:** 64 SERVINGS

¾ cup butter, cubed
1 cup (6 oz.) dark chocolate chips
¾ cup sugar
2 large eggs plus 1 large egg yolk, room temperature
1 tsp. vanilla extract
1 cup all-purpose flour
⅓ cup dark baking cocoa
½ tsp. salt
1 cup Andes creme de menthe baking chips

TOPPING
1 pkg. (8 oz.) cream cheese, softened
½ cup sugar
¼ cup Irish cream liqueur, such as Baileys
1 large egg plus 1 large egg white, room temperature

1. Preheat oven to 350°. Line an 8-in. square baking pan with parchment, letting ends extend up sides. In a large microwave-safe bowl, microwave butter and chocolate chips on high until butter is melted, about 60 seconds. Stir until chocolate is melted. Whisk in sugar. Cool slightly. Whisk in the eggs and yolk, 1 at a time, and vanilla until blended. Stir in flour, baking cocoa and salt; fold in Andes chips. Spread into prepared pan.

2. For the topping, in a large bowl, beat the cream cheese and sugar until smooth. Beat in the liqueur. Add egg and egg white; beat on low speed just until blended. Pour over the brownie layer. Bake until the center is almost set, 45-50 minutes. Cool 1 hour on a wire rack. Refrigerate at least 3 hours or overnight.

3. Lifting with parchment, remove brownies from pan. Cut into 1-in. squares.

1 SQUARE: 96 cal., 6g fat (4g sat. fat), 21mg chol., 54mg sod., 10g carb. (8g sugars, 0 fiber), 1g pro.

Buttery 3-Ingredient Shortbread Cookies

With only a few ingredients, these buttery cookies are so simple to prepare.
An optional dusting of confectioners' sugar provides a sweet touch.
—*Pattie Prescott, Manchester, NH*

PREP: 10 MIN. • BAKE: 30 MIN. + COOLING • MAKES: 16 COOKIES

1 **cup unsalted butter, softened**
½ **cup sugar**
2 **cups all-purpose flour**
   Confectioners' sugar, optional

1. Preheat oven to 325°. Cream butter and sugar until light and fluffy, 5-7 minutes. Gradually beat in the flour. Press dough into an ungreased 9-in. square baking pan. Prick with a fork.

2. Bake until light brown, 30-35 minutes. Cut into squares while warm. Cool completely on a wire rack. If desired, dust with confectioners' sugar.

1 COOKIE: 183 cal., 12g fat (7g sat. fat), 31mg chol., 2mg sod., 18g carb. (6g sugars, 0 fiber), 2g pro.

USE A BETTER BUTTER
With shortbread more than any other cookie, the flavor of the butter determines the flavor, so quality is key. This is the time to splurge on the best butter you can find, such as a European-style butter that has a higher butterfat content.

Chewy Chocolate-Cherry Bars

Colorful dried cherries and pistachios star in this take on seven-layer bars.
To switch it up even more, try cinnamon or chocolate graham cracker
crumbs instead of plain, and substitute pecans or walnuts for the pistachios.
—Taste of Home *Test Kitchen*

PREP: 10 MIN. • **BAKE:** 25 MIN. + COOLING • **MAKES:** 3 DOZEN

1. Preheat oven to 350°. In a small bowl, mix cracker crumbs and butter. Press into a greased 13x9-in. baking pan. In a large bowl, mix the remaining ingredients until blended; carefully spread over crust.

2. Bake 25-28 minutes or until edges are golden brown. Cool completely in pan on a wire rack. Cut into bars.

1 BAR: 164 cal., 9g fat (5g sat. fat), 11mg chol., 77mg sod., 21g carb. (17g sugars, 1g fiber), 2g pro.

1½ cups graham cracker
   crumbs
½ cup butter, melted
1 can (14 oz.) sweetened
   condensed milk
1½ cups dried cherries
1½ cups semisweet
   chocolate chips
1 cup sweetened
   shredded coconut
1 cup pistachios,
   chopped

READER REVIEW

"I love this recipe and the combination of dried cherries and pistachios. It's a great addition to my holiday baking."

—DEBPETERSEN, TASTEOFHOME.COM

Banana Nut Brownies

This recipe comes from my Grandma Schlientz. Any time there are
ripe bananas around our house, it's time to make these brownies!
People are always surprised to learn that bananas are the secret ingredient.
—*Christine Mol, Grand Rapids, MI*

PREP: 10 MIN. • BAKE: 40 MIN. + COOLING • MAKES: 16 BROWNIES

1. In a bowl, combine butter, sugar and cocoa. Stir in eggs, milk and vanilla. Blend in flour, baking powder and salt. Stir in bananas and nuts.

2. Pour into a greased 9-in. square baking pan. Bake at 350° until a toothpick comes out with moist crumbs, 40-45 minutes. Cool completely in pan on a wire rack. Cut into bars. If desired, dust with confectioners' sugar just before serving.

1 BROWNIE: 163 cal., 9g fat (4g sat. fat), 42mg chol., 128mg sod., 20g carb. (15g sugars, 1g fiber), 3g pro.

½ cup butter, melted,
   cooled
1 cup sugar
3 Tbsp. baking cocoa
2 large eggs, room
   temperature,
   lightly beaten
1 Tbsp. 2% milk
1 tsp. vanilla extract
½ cup all-purpose flour
1 tsp. baking powder
¼ tsp. salt
1 cup mashed ripe
   bananas (2½ to
   3 medium)
½ cup chopped walnuts
   Confectioners' sugar,
   optional

GO BANANAS!
Ripe bananas are sweeter than unripe ones and are easier to mash, making them ideal for baking. To make green bananas ripen faster, put them in a paper bag with other ripe fruit (like apples) and fold up the bag. Check on them daily to see if they've ripened enough.

If bananas are ripe but you're not ready to use them yet, place them in a sealed plastic bag in the fridge. The peels will brown but the fruit won't. You can keep them there for 4-5 days.

Mixed Nut Bars

One pan of these bars goes a long way.
They get a nice flavor from butterscotch chips.
—Bobbi Brown, Waupaca, WI

PREP: 10 MIN. • BAKE: 20 MIN. + COOLING • MAKES: 2½ DOZEN

1½ cups all-purpose flour
¾ cup packed brown
   sugar
¼ tsp. salt
½ cup plus 2 Tbsp.
   cold butter, divided
1 cup butterscotch chips
½ cup light corn syrup
1 can (11½ oz.) mixed nuts

1. Preheat oven to 350°. In a small bowl, combine flour, brown sugar and salt. Cut in ½ cup butter until mixture resembles coarse crumbs. Press into a greased 13x9-in. baking pan. Bake for 10 minutes.

2. Meanwhile, in a microwave, melt butterscotch chips and the remaining butter; stir until smooth. Stir in corn syrup.

3. Sprinkle nuts over crust; top with butterscotch mixture. Bake until set, about 10 minutes. Cool completely on a wire rack. Cut into bars.

1 BAR: 201 cal., 12g fat (5g sat. fat), 10mg chol., 98mg sod., 22g carb. (15g sugars, 1g fiber), 3g pro.

Lemony Layer Bars

One of my favorite cakes is a white chocolate cake with coconut lemon filling, dark chocolate frosting and almonds. This version of a seven-layer bar combines all those flavors into an easy-to-eat treat. Using soda cracker crumbs makes the bars a little different.
—*Arlene Erlbach, Morton Grove, IL*

PREP: 20 MIN. • **BAKE:** 25 MIN. + COOLING • **MAKES:** 2 DOZEN

1. Preheat oven to 375°. Line a 13x9-in. baking pan with parchment, letting ends extend up sides. In a large bowl, mix cracker crumbs and butter. Press onto the bottom of prepared pan. Sprinkle with white chips, coconut, almonds and chocolate chips.

2. In a small bowl, combine milk, lemon curd and 1 Tbsp. zest. Pour over chips. Sprinkle with remaining 1 Tbsp. zest. Bake until edges are golden brown, 25-30 minutes. Cool completely in pan on a wire rack. Lifting with the parchment, remove from pan. Cut into bars. Store in an airtight container.

1 BAR: 245 cal., 14g fat (8g sat. fat), 20mg chol., 98mg sod., 27g carb. (21g sugars, 1g fiber), 4g pro.

2 cups crushed unsalted top saltines
½ cup butter, melted
1 cup white baking chips
1 cup sweetened shredded coconut
1 cup coarsely chopped almonds
1 cup (6 oz.) semisweet chocolate chips
1 can (14 oz.) sweetened condensed milk
¼ cup lemon curd
2 Tbsp. grated lemon zest, divided

Pecan Brownies

It's hard to eat just one of these nutty treats.
So it's a good thing a batch can bake up in a matter of minutes!
—*Karen Batchelor, Bellevue, NE*

PREP: 15 MIN. • BAKE: 15 MIN. + COOLING • MAKES: 16 BROWNIES

1. Preheat oven to 350°. In a saucepan over low heat, melt butter and chocolate. Stir in sugar; cool slightly. Add eggs and vanilla; mix well. Stir in flour and pecans.

2. Spread into a greased 8-in. square baking pan. Bake until a toothpick inserted in the center comes out clean, 15-20 minutes. Cool completely on a rack. Cut into bars.

1 BROWNIE: 165 cal., 10g fat (5g sat. fat), 42mg chol., 66mg sod., 18g carb. (12g sugars, 1g fiber), 2g pro.

½ cup butter, cubed
2 oz. unsweetened chocolate, chopped
1 cup sugar
2 large eggs, room temperature, lightly beaten
1 tsp. vanilla extract
¾ cup all-purpose flour
½ to 1 cup chopped pecans

SLOW AND LOW
When melting chocolate, it's important to work slowly over low heat. When exposed to too much heat too fast, chocolate can develop a grainy texture or, worse, it can burn entirely. Also, breaking the bar into small pieces will help the chocolate melt more evenly.

Pomegranate Magic Bars

Pomegranates make desserts festive and bright with a burst of juicy sweetness, especially during the holiday season. These bars are no exception.
—*Lisa Keys, Kennett Square, PA*

PREP: 25 MIN. • BAKE: 45 MIN. + COOLING • MAKES: 3 DOZEN

1¼ cups all-purpose flour
¾ cup sugar
¼ cup baking cocoa
¾ cup cold butter, cubed
1 large egg, room temperature
½ tsp. vanilla extract
1 Tbsp. sesame seeds, toasted
1 cup sweetened shredded coconut, toasted
½ cup slivered almonds, toasted
2 cups (12 oz.) semisweet chocolate chips
1 can (14 oz.) sweetened condensed milk
1 cup pomegranate seeds

1. Preheat the oven to 350°. Line a 13x9-in. pan with parchment, letting ends extend up sides. Lightly grease parchment with cooking spray. In a food processor, combine flour, sugar and cocoa; pulse until combined. Add butter; pulse until mixture appears sandy. Add egg and vanilla; pulse just until combined. Press the dough into prepared pan.

2. Sprinkle the dough with sesame seeds. Bake until top appears dry and a toothpick inserted in the center comes out clean, 20-25 minutes. Remove from oven; sprinkle evenly with the coconut, almonds and chocolate chips. Pour condensed milk evenly over the top; return to oven. Bake until golden brown, 25-30 minutes. Cool on wire rack 10 minutes.

3. Sprinkle with pomegranate seeds; press gently into warm topping with back of a spoon. Cool completely in pan on wire rack. Lifting with parchment, remove from pan. Cut into bars.

1 BAR: 176 cal., 10g fat (6g sat. fat), 19mg chol., 55mg sod., 22g carb. (17g sugars, 1g fiber), 3g pro.

Winning Cranberry Date Bars

I enjoy making these when the cranberry season arrives. The recipe is very easy to put together, which is perfect for busy parents like me.
—*Richard Grams, LaCrosse, WI*

PREP: 20 MIN. • BAKE: 30 MIN. + COOLING • MAKES: 4 DOZEN

1. Preheat oven to 350°. In a large saucepan, combine cranberries and dates. Cover and cook over low heat until berries pop, 15 minutes, stirring often. Remove from the heat and stir in vanilla; set aside.

2. In a large bowl, combine flour, oats, brown sugar, baking soda and salt. Stir in butter until crumbly. Press half into an ungreased 13x9-in. baking pan. Bake 8 minutes. Spoon cranberry mixture over the crust; spread gently. Sprinkle with remaining crumb mixture; pat down gently.

3. Bake until golden brown, 20-25 minutes. Cool completely in the pan on a wire rack. Combine glaze ingredients; drizzle over top. Cut into bars.

1 BAR: 128 cal., 4g fat (2g sat fat), 10mg chol., 58mg sod., 22g carb. (15g sugars, 1g fiber), 1g pro.

1 **pkg. (12 oz.) fresh or frozen cranberries**
1 **pkg. (8 oz.) chopped dates**
1 **tsp. vanilla extract**
2 **cups all-purpose flour**
2 **cups quick-cooking oats**
1½ **cups packed brown sugar**
½ **tsp. baking soda**
¼ **tsp. salt**
1 **cup butter, melted**

ORANGE GLAZE
2 **cups confectioners' sugar**
2 **to 3 Tbsp. orange juice**
½ **tsp. vanilla extract**

Chocolate Chip Blondies

Folks who adore chocolate chip cookies will enjoy that same beloved flavor in these golden bars. They can be mixed up in a jiffy, taste wonderful and are perfect for occasions when company drops by unexpectedly or you need a treat in a hurry.
—*Rhonda Knight, Hecker, IL*

PREP: 10 MIN. • BAKE: 20 MIN. + COOLING • MAKES: 3 DOZEN

1. In a large bowl, combine brown sugar, butter, eggs and vanilla just until blended. Combine flour, baking powder and salt; add to brown sugar mixture. Stir in chips.

2. Spread into a greased 13x9-in. baking pan. Bake at 350° until a toothpick inserted in the center comes out clean, 18-20 minutes. Cool completely on a wire rack. Cut into bars.

1 BLONDIE: 102 cal., 4g fat (2g sat. fat), 19mg chol., 72mg sod., 16g carb. (12g sugars, 0 fiber), 1g pro.

1½ cups packed brown sugar
½ cup butter, melted
2 large eggs, lightly beaten, room temperature
1 tsp. vanilla extract
1½ cups all-purpose flour
½ tsp. baking powder
½ tsp. salt
1 cup semisweet chocolate chips

SWEET SWAPS
You can make these blondies your own by swapping out the semisweet chocolate chips for white baking chips. Or amp up the crunch by stirring in a handful of chopped walnuts or pecans.

Coconut Nutella Brownies

When my parents were coming over for dinner one night, I wanted a fast go-to brownie. My mom loves coconut and chocolate, and I knew this would be the perfect treat.

—*Danielle Lee, West Palm Beach, FL*

PREP: 15 MIN. • BAKE: 25 MIN. + COOLING • MAKES: 2 DOZEN

½ cup butter, softened
1⅓ cups sugar
½ cup Nutella
4 large eggs, room temperature
1 tsp. vanilla extract
1 cup all-purpose flour
½ cup whole wheat flour
⅔ cup Dutch-processed cocoa
½ cup flaked coconut
½ cup old-fashioned oats

1. Preheat oven to 350°. In a large bowl, beat butter, sugar and Nutella until blended. Add eggs, 1 at a time, beating well after each addition. Beat in vanilla. In another bowl, whisk flours and cocoa; gradually beat into butter mixture, mixing well. Fold in the coconut and oats. Spread into a greased 13x9-in. baking pan.

2. Bake until a toothpick comes out with moist crumbs, 22-25 minutes (do not overbake). Cool completely in pan on a wire rack. Cut into bars.

1 BROWNIE: 186 cal., 9g fat (5g sat. fat), 41mg chol., 50mg sod., 26g carb. (16g sugars, 4g fiber), 4g pro.

NOTES

Butter Pecan Bars with Penuche Drizzle

I have made these bars for many, many years. They are rich, chewy and buttery—all the good stuff. I like to use dark brown sugar for extra flavor. A sprinkle of some pecans on the top makes for a nice nutty, toasted flavor.
—*Kallee Krong-McCreery, Escondido, CA*

PREP: 30 MIN. • BAKE: 25 MIN. + COOLING • MAKES: 2 DOZEN

2 **cups packed dark brown sugar**
½ **cup butter, melted**
2 **large eggs, room temperature**
1 **Tbsp. vanilla extract**
2 **cups all-purpose flour**
½ **tsp. salt**
1 **cup chopped pecans, divided**

ICING
3 **Tbsp. butter**
¼ **cup packed dark brown sugar**
1 **Tbsp. 2% milk**
½ **cup confectioners' sugar**

1. Preheat oven to 350°. In a large bowl, beat the brown sugar and butter until blended. Beat in eggs and vanilla. In another bowl, whisk the flour and salt; gradually beat into sugar mixture. Stir in ¾ cup pecans. Pour into a greased 13x9-in. baking pan; sprinkle with remaining ¼ cup pecans.

2. Bake until a toothpick inserted in center comes out clean (do not overbake). Cool completely in pan on a wire rack.

3. For icing, in a small saucepan, melt butter over low heat. Stir in brown sugar; cook and stir 30 seconds. Add milk; cook and stir 30 seconds. Remove from heat; whisk in confectioners' sugar until smooth. Immediately drizzle over bars; let stand until set. Cut into bars.

1 BAR: 212 cal., 9g fat (4g sat. fat), 30mg chol., 103mg sod., 32g carb. (23g sugars, 1g fiber), 2g pro.

Almond Poppy Seed Bars

These tender squares have a sweet frosting and generous sprinkling of poppy seeds throughout. They're a snap to whip up with ingredients I usually have on hand.
—*Pam Mroz, Rochester, MN*

PREP: 20 MIN. • BAKE: 20 MIN. + COOLING • MAKES: ABOUT 5½ DOZEN

1. In a bowl, beat the eggs, sugar, milk, oil, extracts and butter flavoring. Combine the flour, poppy seeds, baking powder and salt; add to the egg mixture and mix just until combined. Spread into a greased 15x10x1-in. baking pan.

2. Bake at 350° for 20 minutes or until a toothpick inserted in the center comes out clean. Cool completely in the pan on a wire rack.

3. In a bowl, combine the frosting ingredients; beat until smooth. Frost before cutting into bars.

1 SERVING: 115 cal., 5g fat (1g sat. fat), 13mg chol., 78mg sod., 17g carb. (12g sugars, 0 fiber), 1g pro

READER REVIEW
"These bars are great! I didn't even need the frosting."
—PAWMARTIN, TASTEOFHOME.COM

 3 large eggs, room
    temperature
2¼ cups sugar
1½ cups 2% milk
 1 cup canola oil
1½ tsp. almond extract
1½ tsp. vanilla extract
1½ tsp. butter flavoring
    or additional vanilla
    extract
 3 cups all-purpose flour
4½ tsp. poppy seeds
1½ tsp. baking powder
1½ tsp. salt

FROSTING
 3 cups confectioners'
    sugar
⅓ cup butter, melted
 3 Tbsp. milk

Angel Wings

I knew this crisp roll-up cookie was a winner when my sister first sampled one.
She was so impressed, she asked me to bake her wedding cake!
—*R. Lane, Tenafly, NJ*

PREP: 30 MIN. + CHILLING • **BAKE:** 20 MIN. • **MAKES:** ABOUT 3 DOZEN

1 cup cold butter, cubed
1½ cups all-purpose flour
½ cup sour cream
10 Tbsp. sugar, divided
3 tsp. ground cinnamon, divided
Coarse sugar, optional

1. In a large bowl, cut butter into flour until the mixture resembles coarse crumbs. Stir in the sour cream. Turn onto a lightly floured surface; knead 6-8 times or until mixture holds together. Shape into 4 balls; flatten slightly. Wrap; refrigerate for 4 hours or overnight.

2. Unwrap 1 ball. Sprinkle 2 Tbsp. sugar on waxed paper; coat all sides of the ball with sugar. Roll into a 12x5-in. rectangle between 2 sheets of waxed paper. Remove the top sheet of waxed paper. Sprinkle dough with ¾ tsp. cinnamon. Lightly mark a line down the center of the dough, making two 6x5-in. rectangles.

3. Starting with a short side, roll up jelly-roll style to the center mark; peel waxed paper away while rolling. Repeat with other short side. Securely wrap in waxed paper; freeze for 30 minutes. Repeat with remaining balls of dough.

4. Place the remaining sugar or, if desired, coarse sugar on waxed paper. Unwrap 1 roll. Cut into ½-in. slices; dip each side into the sugar. Place 2 in. apart on ungreased baking sheets.

5. Bake at 375° until golden brown, 16-18 minutes. Remove to wire racks to cool.

1 COOKIE: 85 cal., 6g fat (4g sat. fat), 14mg chol., 42mg sod., 8g carb. (4g sugars, 0 fiber), 1g pro.

Toffee Cranberry Crisps

I've had more friends request this recipe than any other cookie recipe I bake. The combination of cranberries, chocolate chips and toffee bits is wonderful.
—*Ann Quaerna, Lake Geneva, WI*

PREP: 15 MIN. + CHILLING • **BAKE:** 10 MIN./BATCH • **MAKES:** 4 DOZEN

1 cup butter, softened
¾ cup sugar
¾ cup packed
   brown sugar
1 large egg, room
   temperature
1 tsp. vanilla extract
1½ cups all-purpose flour
1½ cups quick-cooking
   oats
1 tsp. baking soda
¼ tsp. salt
1 cup dried cranberries
1 cup miniature
   semisweet
   chocolate chips
1 cup milk chocolate
   English toffee bits

1. In a large bowl, cream butter and sugars until light and fluffy, 5-7 minutes. Beat in egg and vanilla. Combine the flour, oats, baking soda and salt; gradually add to creamed mixture and mix well. Stir in cranberries, chocolate chips and toffee bits.

2. Shape into three 8-in. rolls; securely wrap each in waxed paper. Refrigerate 2 hours or until firm.

3. Preheat oven to 350°. Unwrap rolls and cut into ½-in. slices. Place slices 2 in. apart on lightly greased baking sheets. Bake for 8-10 minutes or until golden brown. Remove to wire racks to cool.

1 COOKIE: 139 cal., 7g fat (4g sat. fat), 16mg chol., 89mg sod., 19g carb. (14g sugars, 1g fiber), 1g pro.

READER REVIEW
"This is a delicious and easy recipe. I used dried cherries rather than cranberries, and they were a big hit."
—COUNTRYPATTY, TASTEOFHOME.COM

Holiday Sugar Cookies

I add a hint of lemon to these delightful sugar cookies. I love to put a
simple tree design on each one, but you can decorate as you like.
—*Katie Koziolek, Hartland, MN*

PREP: 25 MIN. + CHILLING • **BAKE:** 10 MIN./BATCH + COOLING • **MAKES:** ABOUT 9½ DOZEN

1. In a large bowl, cream butter and sugar until light and
fluffy, 5-7 minutes. Add eggs, 1 at a time, beating well after
each addition. Beat in lemon zest and vanilla. Combine
flour and baking soda; gradually add to creamed mixture
and mix well. Shape into three 10-in. rolls; wrap each
in waxed paper. Refrigerate for 4 hours or until firm.

2. Preheat oven to 350°. Unwrap rolls and cut into ¼-in.
slices. Place slices 2 in. apart on ungreased baking sheets.
Bake until edges are lightly browned, 10-15 minutes.
Remove to wire racks to cool completely.

2 **cups butter, softened**
2 **cups sugar**
3 **large eggs, room**
   temperature
1 **Tbsp. grated**
   lemon zest
2 **tsp. vanilla extract**
6 **cups all-purpose flour**
1 **tsp. baking soda**

3. In a large bowl, combine the confectioners' sugar, butter,
milk and food coloring until smooth. Transfer to a pastry
bag fitted with a small tip; drizzle over cookies in the
shape of a Christmas tree. Place 1 Red Hot at the top of
each tree.

FREEZE OPTION: Freeze dough for up to 3 months. To use,
thaw in refrigerator before slicing, baking and decorating
as directed.

FROSTING
3 **cups confectioners'**
   sugar
3 **Tbsp. butter, melted**
¼ **cup 2% milk**
   Green food coloring
   Red Hots

1 COOKIE: 169 cal., 7g fat (4g sat. fat), 30mg chol., 97mg sod.,
24g carb. (13g sugars, 0 fiber), 2g pro.

ON A ROLL
To prevent the roll of dough from becoming flat on one
side as it sits in the fridge, turn to an empty cardboard
paper towel roll. Just cut the roll lengthwise and place
the wrapped dough inside.

Ribbon Icebox Cookies

Three ribbons of flavor—cherry, chocolate and poppy seed—combine into one tender Neapolitan-style cookie. My mom made these when we were kids. They are so good.
—*Karlyne Moreau, Yakima, WA*

PREP: 25 MIN. + CHILLING • BAKE: 10 MIN. • MAKES: 20 COOKIES

½ cup shortening
⅔ cup sugar
2 Tbsp. beaten egg, room temperature
½ tsp. vanilla extract
1¼ cups all-purpose flour
¾ tsp. baking powder
¼ tsp. salt
2 Tbsp. red candied cherries, chopped
½ oz. unsweetened chocolate, melted
2 tsp. poppy seeds

1. Line a 5x3x2-in. loaf pan with waxed paper; set aside. In a small bowl, cream shortening and sugar until light and fluffy, 5-7 minutes. Beat in egg and vanilla. Combine flour, baking powder and salt; gradually add to creamed mixture and mix well.

2. Divide dough into thirds. Add cherries to 1 portion; spread evenly into prepared pan. Add melted chocolate to second portion; spread evenly over first layer. Add poppy seeds to third portion; spread over second layer. Cover with waxed paper; refrigerate overnight.

3. Preheat oven to 375°. Remove dough from pan and cut into ¼-in. slices. Place 1 in. apart on ungreased baking sheets. Bake for 8-9 minutes or until lightly browned. Cool 1 minute before removing to wire racks.

1 COOKIE: 109 cal., 6g fat (2g sat. fat), 6mg chol., 48mg sod., 14g carb. (7g sugars, 0 fiber), 1g pro.

Glazed Italian Fruitcake Cookies

I grew up in Italy eating these every Christmas. I have such fond memories that I make them every year and give them to friends.
—*Trisha Kruse, Eagle, ID*

PREP: 25 MIN. + CHILLING • **BAKE:** 10 MIN./BATCH + COOLING • **MAKES:** 4 DOZEN

- 1 cup butter, softened
- ⅓ cup half-and-half cream
- 1 tsp. vanilla extract
- 3 cups all-purpose flour
- ¾ cup sugar
- 4 tsp. baking powder
- ½ tsp. salt
- ½ cup chopped walnuts, toasted
- ½ cup chopped mixed dried fruit

GLAZE
- 1 oz. unsweetened chocolate
- 1½ tsp. butter
- 1 cup confectioners' sugar
- ½ tsp. vanilla extract
- 2 to 3 Tbsp. 2% milk

1. In a large bowl, beat butter, cream and vanilla until blended. In another bowl, whisk flour, sugar, baking powder and salt; gradually beat into creamed mixture. Stir in walnuts and dried fruit (mixture will be crumbly). Press mixture together to form a ball.

2. Divide dough in half; shape each into a 6-in.-long roll. Wrap each in waxed paper. Place wrapped rolls in airtight containers. Refrigerate 1 hour or until firm.

3. Preheat oven to 350°. Unwrap dough and cut crosswise into ¼-in. slices. Place 1 in. apart on ungreased baking sheets. Bake 10-12 minutes or until edges are light brown. Remove from pans to wire racks to cool completely.

4. In a large heavy saucepan, melt chocolate and butter over low heat. Gradually stir in confectioners' sugar, vanilla and enough milk to reach drizzling consistency. Remove from heat; drizzle over cooled cookies.

FREEZE OPTION: Place wrapped rolls in a freezer container; freeze. To use, unwrap frozen rolls and cut into slices. If necessary, let dough stand 15 minutes at room temperature before cutting. Bake as directed.

1 COOKIE: 106 cal., 5g fat (3g sat. fat), 11mg chol., 100mg sod., 13g carb. (7g sugars, 0 fiber), 1g pro.

Lemon Lover's Cookies

These light cookies will melt in your mouth.
They're sure to be a hit wherever you serve them.
—*Virginia Dillard, Whitmire, SC*

PREP: 20 MIN. + CHILLING • BAKE: 10 MIN./BATCH + COOLING • MAKES: ABOUT 3½ DOZEN

¾ cup butter, softened
⅓ cup confectioners' sugar
2 tsp. lemon juice
1 cup all-purpose flour
½ cup cornstarch
1 tsp. grated lemon zest

LEMON FROSTING
¼ cup butter, softened
1 cup confectioners' sugar
2 tsp. lemon juice
1 tsp. grated lemon zest

GARNISH
Additional grated lemon zest, optional

1. In a small bowl, cream butter and sugar until light and fluffy, 5-7 minutes. Beat in lemon juice. Combine the flour, cornstarch and lemon zest; gradually add to creamed mixture and mix well.

2. Shape into a 1½-in.-diameter roll; securely wrap in waxed paper. Refrigerate for 1 hour or until firm.

3. Preheat oven to 350°. Unwrap dough and cut into ¼-in. slices. Place slices 2 in. apart on greased baking sheets. Bake for 10-12 minutes or until edges are golden brown. Gently remove to wire racks to cool completely.

4. For frosting, in a small bowl, beat butter until fluffy. Add the confectioners' sugar, lemon juice and zest; beat until smooth. Spread over the cooled cookies; sprinkle with additional lemon zest if desired. Let stand until set. Store in an airtight container.

1 COOKIE: 74 cal., 5g fat (3g sat. fat), 12mg chol., 37mg sod., 8g carb. (4g sugars, 0 fiber), 0 pro. **DIABETIC EXCHANGES:** 1 fat, ½ starch.

Simply Sesames

My kitchen counter is covered with these crispy crowd-pleasers at Christmastime. I make them for friends and family. I also add them to care packages our church delivers to area senior citizens.
—*Jennifer Lynn, Kamiah, ID*

PREP: 20 MIN. + CHILLING • **BAKE:** 20 MIN./BATCH + COOLING • **MAKES:** ABOUT 3½ DOZEN

1 cup butter, softened
¾ cup sugar
1½ cups all-purpose flour
1 cup sweetened shredded coconut
½ cup sesame seeds
¼ cup finely chopped almonds

1. In a bowl, cream butter and sugar until light and fluffy, 5-7 minutes. Add flour; mix just until combined. Stir in coconut, sesame seeds and almonds. Chill for 15 minutes.

2. Divide the dough in half. Shape each portion into a 2-in.-diameter roll. Securely wrap each roll in waxed paper. Refrigerate 2 hours or overnight.

3. Preheat oven to 300°. Remove the waxed paper. Cut dough into ¼-in. slices; place on ungreased baking sheets. Bake for 20-25 minutes or until lightly browned. Cool 2 minutes; remove to wire racks to cool completely.

1 COOKIE: 94 cal., 6g fat (4g sat. fat), 12mg chol., 41mg sod., 9g carb. (5g sugars, 1g fiber), 1g pro.

Two-Tone Christmas Cookies

I dreamed up this recipe using two of my favorite flavors: pistachio and raspberry. The pink and green cookies are tasty and eye-catching too. They're perfect for formal or informal gatherings, and everybody likes them.
—*Marie Capobianco, Portsmouth, RI*

PREP: 25 MIN. + CHILLING • **BAKE:** 10 MIN./BATCH + COOLING • **MAKES:** 6½ DOZEN

- 1 **cup butter, softened**
- 1½ **cups sugar**
- 2 **large egg yolks, room temperature**
- 2 **tsp. vanilla extract**
- 1 **tsp. almond extract**
- 3½ **cups all-purpose flour**
- 1 **tsp. salt**
- 1 **tsp. baking powder**
- ½ **tsp. baking soda**
- 9 **drops green food coloring**
- 1 **Tbsp. 2% milk**
- ⅓ **cup finely chopped pistachios**
- 9 **drops red food coloring**
- 3 **Tbsp. seedless raspberry preserves**
- 2 **cups semisweet chocolate chips, melted**
- **Additional chopped pistachios, optional**

1. In a large bowl, cream butter and sugar until light and fluffy, 5-7 minutes. Beat in the egg yolks and extracts. Combine the flour, salt, baking powder and baking soda; gradually add to creamed mixture and mix well. Divide dough in half. Stir green food coloring, milk and nuts into 1 portion; mix well. Add red food coloring and jam to the other half.

2. Between 2 pieces of waxed paper, shape each portion of dough into an 8x6-in. rectangle. Cut in half lengthwise. Place 1 green rectangle on another piece of waxed paper. Top with 1 pink rectangle; press together lightly. Repeat, forming a second stack. Wrap each in waxed paper and place in an airtight container; refrigerate overnight.

3. Preheat oven to 375°. Remove 1 stack of dough from the refrigerator at a time. Unwrap dough; cut in half lengthwise. Return 1 portion to the refrigerator. Cut remaining portion into ⅛-in. slices. Place 1 in. apart on ungreased baking sheets. Bake for 7-9 minutes or until set. Remove to wire racks to cool completely. Repeat with the remaining dough.

4. Drizzle cooled cookies with melted chocolate. Sprinkle with additional pistachios if desired.

1 COOKIE: 27 cal., 1g fat (1g sat. fat), 4mg chol., 22mg sod., 4g carb. (2g sugars, 0 fiber), 0 pro.

Cherry Christmas Slices

Brilliant red and green candied cherries add extra sparkle to these delicious holiday cookies. What I really like best is that this recipe is easy to mix up ahead of time. In fact, I've often made the dough in November and kept it in the freezer until I needed it in December!
—*Katie Koziolek, Hartland, MN*

PREP: 20 MIN. + CHILLING • BAKE: 10 MIN. • MAKES: ABOUT 11 DOZEN

1. In a large bowl, cream the butter and sugar until light and fluffy, 5-7 minutes. Beat in the egg and vanilla. Add flour; mix well. Stir in cherries and pecans. Cover and chill 1 hour.

2. Shape dough into three 6-in.-long rolls; wrap securely and place in a freezer container. Freeze up to 2 months.

3. To bake, cut frozen rolls into ⅛-in. slices and place on ungreased baking sheets. Bake at 325° until edges are golden brown, 10-12 minutes. Cool on wire racks.

1 cup butter, softened
1 cup confectioners' sugar
1 large egg, room temperature
1 tsp. vanilla extract
2¼ cups all-purpose flour
1 cup red candied cherries, halved
1 cup green candied cherries, halved
1 cup pecan halves

1 COOKIE: 37 cal., 2g fat (1g sat. fat), 5mg chol., 14mg sod., 5g carb. (3g sugars, 0 fiber), 0 pro.

NOTES

_____
_____
_____
_____
_____
_____
_____
_____

Ginger & Maple Macadamia Nut Cookies

This spiced cookie has a real kick of ginger that reminds me of the traditional German lebkuchen. Add colored sprinkles for extra sparkle.
—*Thomas Faglon, Somerset, NJ*

PREP: 45 MIN. + CHILLING • BAKE: 10 MIN./BATCH + COOLING • MAKES: ABOUT 7 DOZEN

- 1½ cups butter, softened
- ½ cup sugar
- ¾ cup maple syrup
- 4 cups all-purpose flour
- 3 tsp. ground ginger
- 3 tsp. ground cinnamon
- 1 tsp. ground allspice
- ½ tsp. ground cloves
- 1½ tsp. salt
- 1½ tsp. baking soda
- 1½ cups finely chopped macadamia nuts
- 24 oz. dark chocolate candy coating, melted
- ⅓ cup finely chopped crystallized ginger

1. In a large bowl, cream butter and sugar until light and fluffy, 5-7 minutes. Gradually beat in syrup. In another bowl, whisk flour, spices, salt and baking soda; gradually beat into creamed mixture. Stir in nuts.

2. Divide dough in half; shape each into a 12-in.-long roll. Wrap securely; refrigerate 2 hours or until firm.

3. Preheat oven to 350°. Unwrap and cut dough crosswise into ¼-in. slices. Place 1 in. apart on ungreased baking sheets. Bake for 8-10 minutes or until set. Cool on pans 2 minutes. Remove to wire racks to cool completely.

4. Dip each cookie halfway into the melted candy coating; allow the excess to drip off. Place on waxed paper-lined baking sheets; sprinkle with the crystallized ginger. Refrigerate until set.

1 COOKIE: 126 cal., 8g fat (4g sat. fat), 9mg chol., 103mg sod., 14g carb. (9g sugars, 1g fiber), 1g pro.

Bite-Sized Cinnamon Roll Cookies

If you love cinnamon rolls and spiced cookies, make a bite-sized
version that combines the best of both worlds. Genius!
—*Jasmine Sheth, New York, NY*

PREP: 1 HOUR + CHILLING • **BAKE:** 10 MIN./BATCH + COOLING • **MAKES:** 6 DOZEN

½ **cup packed
    brown sugar**
4 **tsp. ground cinnamon**
1¼ **cups butter, softened**
4 **oz. cream cheese,
    softened**
1½ **cups sugar**
2 **large eggs, room
    temperature**
2 **tsp. vanilla extract**
2 **tsp. grated orange zest**
4¼ **cups all-purpose flour**
1 **tsp. baking powder**
1 **tsp. active dry yeast**
½ **tsp. salt**

GLAZE
1 **cup confectioners'
    sugar**
2 **Tbsp. 2% milk**
1 **tsp. vanilla extract**

1. In a small bowl, mix brown sugar and cinnamon until
blended. In a large bowl, cream butter, cream cheese
and sugar until light and fluffy, 5-7 minutes. Beat in the
eggs, vanilla and orange zest. In another bowl, whisk
flour, baking powder, yeast and salt; gradually beat into
creamed mixture.

2. Divide dough into 4 portions; chill for 30 minutes or
until no longer sticky. On a lightly floured surface, roll
each into an 8x6-in. rectangle; sprinkle with about
2 Tbsp. brown sugar mixture. Roll up tightly jelly-roll
style, starting with a long side. Wrap in waxed paper;
refrigerate 1 hour or until firm.

3. Preheat oven to 350°. Unwrap dough; cut crosswise into
³⁄₈-in. slices. Place 1 in. apart on greased baking sheets.
Bake for 8-10 minutes or until bottoms are light brown.
Remove from pans to wire racks to cool completely.

4. Whisk glaze ingredients. Dip tops of cookies in glaze.
Let stand until set. Store in an airtight container.

1 COOKIE: 92 cal., 4g fat (2g sat. fat), 16mg chol., 52mg sod.,
13g carb. (7g sugars, 0 fiber), 1g pro.

Coconut Slice & Bake Cookies

Festively tinted flaky coconut reminds me of snowflakes falling under holiday lights. The reds and greens add a little Christmas joy to any cookie tray.
—*Lee Roberts, Racine, WI*

PREP: 25 MIN. + CHILLING • BAKE: 15 MIN./BATCH • MAKES: ABOUT 4½ DOZEN

3 cups sweetened shredded coconut, divided
15 drops red food coloring
10 drops green food coloring
1 cup butter, softened
¾ cup sugar
2 cups all-purpose flour

1. To tint coconut, place 1 cup coconut in each of 2 large bowls. Add red food coloring to 1 bowl; cover and shake or toss to coat. Repeat with remaining coconut and green food coloring.

2. In a large bowl, cream butter and sugar until light and fluffy, 5-7 minutes; gradually beat in the flour. Stir in the remaining coconut. Divide dough in half.

3. Shape 1 portion of dough into a 7-in.-long roll; roll in red coconut, pressing firmly to help adhere. Wrap securely. Repeat with the remaining dough and green coconut. Refrigerate 1-2 hours or until firm.

4. Preheat oven to 325°. Unwrap and cut dough crosswise into ¼-in. slices. Place 1 in. apart on ungreased baking sheets. Bake 12-14 minutes or until bottoms are light brown. Remove from pans to wire racks to cool.

1 COOKIE: 84 cal., 5g fat (4g sat. fat), 9mg chol., 41mg sod., 9g carb. (5g sugars, 0 fiber), 1g pro.

Icebox Spice Cookies

These slice-and-bake cookies become very crispy after they've cooled.
They're wonderful dunked into a cup of coffee or milk.
—*Caroline Smid, Winnipeg, MB*

PREP: 45 MIN. + CHILLING • BAKE: 10 MIN./BATCH • MAKES: 6 DOZEN

1¼ cups butter, softened
1 cup sugar
1 cup packed brown
    sugar
2 large eggs, room
    temperature
3¾ cups all-purpose flour
2 tsp. ground cinnamon
1 tsp. baking soda
1 tsp. salt
1 tsp. ground cloves
1 tsp. ground allspice

1. In a large bowl, cream butter and sugars until light and fluffy, 5-7 minutes. Add eggs, 1 at a time, beating well after each addition. Combine flour, cinnamon, baking soda, salt, cloves and allspice; gradually add to creamed mixture and mix well.

2. Shape into three 6-in. rolls; wrap separately. Refrigerate for at least 2 hours or until firm.

3. Preheat oven to 350°. Unwrap dough and cut into ¼-in. slices. Place 2 in. apart on greased baking sheets. Bake 8-10 minutes or until lightly browned around the edges. Cool 1-2 minutes before removing to wire racks.

1 COOKIE: 76 cal., 3g fat (2g sat. fat), 14mg chol., 86mg sod., 11g carb. (6g sugars, 0 fiber), 1g pro.

CITRUS FROSTING ADDS ZEST!
For added flavor, top these cookies with a little lemon frosting. Cream 2 cups confectioners' sugar, 3 Tbsp. softened butter and 1 tsp. grated lemon zest. Gradually add 3-4 Tbsp. lemon juice, beating until the frosting achieves desired spreading consistency.

Peppermint Candy Cookies

Taking a cue from Star Mints, I created a buttery cookie with a holiday look.
This one melts in your mouth faster than its candy cousin.
—*Gloria McKenzie, Panama City, FL*

PREP: 25 MIN. • **BAKE:** 10 MIN./BATCH • **MAKES:** ABOUT 4 DOZEN

1¼ **cups butter, softened**
¾ **cup confectioners'**
   sugar
2½ **cups all-purpose flour**
½ **tsp. salt**
½ **tsp. peppermint extract**
   Green and red paste or
   gel food coloring

1. In a large bowl, cream butter and confectioners' sugar until light and fluffy. Add flour, salt and extract; mix well. Divide dough into 4 portions. Tint 1 portion green and 1 red; leave remaining portions plain.

2. Divide each portion into thirds; shape each into a 6-in. roll. Flatten into triangular logs, bending the top of 1 point slightly (to give the finished cookies a pinwheel effect). Assemble 1 large roll by alternating 3 green and 3 plain logs. Wrap in waxed paper. Repeat with red and remaining plain dough. Refrigerate 4 hours or until firm.

3. Preheat oven to 375°. Unwrap dough and cut into ¼-in. slices. Place 2 in. apart on ungreased baking sheets. Bake 8-10 minutes or until edges are golden brown. Cool on pans 1 minute. Remove to wire racks to cool.

4. If desired, cut 6-in. square pieces of cellophane or plastic wrap to wrap each cookie; twist ends securely or tie with ribbon.

1 COOKIE: 146 cal., 10g fat (6g sat. fat), 26mg chol., 146mg sod., 14g carb. (4g sugars, 0 fiber), 1g pro.

Mango Fudge
Refrigerator Ribbon Cookies

A ribbon cookie is especially nice because although it's a single snack, it really tastes like two or three different cookies because of its lovely layers. These refrigerated cookies have a rich chocolate layer balanced by a bright orange-mango layer—a special combination.
—*Jeanne Holt, St. Paul, MN*

PREP: 30 MIN. + CHILLING • BAKE: 10 MIN./BATCH • MAKES: 4 DOZEN

1 cup butter, softened
1 cup sugar
1 large egg, room temperature
2 Tbsp. 2% milk
1½ tsp. vanilla extract
3 cups all-purpose flour
1½ tsp. baking powder
½ tsp. salt
½ cup 60% cacao bittersweet chocolate baking chips, melted and cooled
⅓ cup miniature semisweet chocolate chips
½ cup finely chopped dried mango
⅓ cup finely chopped pistachios
2 tsp. grated orange zest

1. In a large bowl, cream butter and sugar until light and fluffy, 5-7 minutes. Beat in egg, milk and vanilla. In another bowl, whisk together the flour, baking powder and salt; gradually add to creamed mixture.

2. Divide dough in half. Mix melted chocolate into 1 half; stir in miniature chips. Mix mango, pistachios and orange zest into the remaining dough.

3. Line an 8x4-in. loaf pan with waxed paper, letting the ends extend over sides. Press half the chocolate dough onto the bottom of pan; top with half the mango dough. Repeat layers.

4. Lifting with waxed paper, remove dough from pan; fold paper over dough to wrap completely. Refrigerate dough in pan until firm, 2 hours or overnight.

5. Preheat oven to 375°. Unwrap and cut dough crosswise into ½-in.-thick slices; cut each slice crosswise into thirds. Place 2 in. apart on ungreased baking sheets.

6. Bake until the edges are lightly browned, 10-12 minutes. Remove from pans to wire racks to cool.

1 COOKIE: 104 cal., 5g fat (3g sat. fat), 14mg chol., 58mg sod., 13g carb. (7g sugars, 1g fiber), 1g pro.

Cherry Cranberry Pinwheels

With the combination of cranberries, cherries, orange zest and cinnamon, these festive cookies are as fragrant as they are flavorful.
—*Deb Perry, Bluffton, IN*

PREP: 1 HOUR + CHILLING • BAKE: 10 MIN./BATCH • MAKES: 4½ DOZEN

1½ cups dried cranberries
1 jar (10 oz.) cherry spreadable fruit
¼ cup water
½ tsp. ground cinnamon

DOUGH
¼ cup butter, softened
1¼ cups sugar
3 large egg whites, room temperature
3 Tbsp. canola oil
2 Tbsp. fat-free milk
2 tsp. vanilla extract
1½ tsp. grated orange zest
3⅓ cups all-purpose flour
¾ tsp. baking powder
½ tsp. ground cinnamon
⅛ tsp. baking soda

1. For filling, combine the first 4 ingredients in a small saucepan. Cook and stir over medium heat for 8 minutes or until liquid is absorbed and cranberries are softened. Remove from the heat; cool slightly. Transfer to a blender; cover and process until smooth. Transfer to a bowl; cover and refrigerate until chilled.

2. For dough, in a large bowl, beat the butter and sugar for 2 minutes or until crumbly. Beat in the egg whites, oil, milk, vanilla and orange zest. Combine the flour, baking powder, cinnamon and baking soda; gradually add to sugar mixture and mix well.

3. Divide dough in half. On a floured surface, roll 1 portion of dough into a 14x9-in. rectangle. Spread with half the filling. Roll up jelly-roll style, starting with a long side. Repeat with remaining dough and filling. Wrap each roll in waxed paper; refrigerate at least 4 hours.

4. Preheat oven to 375°. Unwrap dough; cut into ½-in. slices. Place 2 in. apart on greased baking sheets. Bake for 10-12 minutes or until the bottoms are lightly browned (do not overbake). Remove to wire racks to cool.

1 COOKIE: 83 cal., 2g fat (1g sat. fat), 2mg chol., 21mg sod., 16g carb. (9g sugars, 0 fiber), 1g pro. **DIABETIC EXCHANGES:** 1 starch, ½ fat.

Air-Fryer Lemon Slice Sugar Cookies

Here's a refreshing variation on my grandmother's sugar cookie recipe. Lemon pudding mix and icing add a subtle tartness that tingles your taste buds.
—*Melissa Turkington, Camano Island, WA*

PREP: 15 MIN. + CHILLING • **COOK:** 10 MIN./ BATCH + COOLING • **MAKES:** ABOUT 2 DOZEN

½ **cup unsalted butter, softened**
1 **pkg. (3.4 oz.) instant lemon pudding mix**
½ **cup sugar**
1 **large egg, room temperature**
2 **Tbsp. 2% milk**
1½ **cups all-purpose flour**
1 **tsp. baking powder**
¼ **tsp. salt**

ICING
⅔ **cup confectioners' sugar**
2 **to 4 tsp. lemon juice**

1. In a large bowl, cream butter, pudding mix and sugar until light and fluffy, 5-7 minutes. Beat in egg and milk. In another bowl, whisk flour, baking powder and salt; gradually beat into creamed mixture.

2. Divide the dough in half. On a lightly floured surface, shape each into a 6-in.-long roll. Wrap and refrigerate 3 hours or until firm.

3. Preheat air fryer to 325°. Unwrap and cut the dough crosswise into ½-in. slices. In batches, place slices in a single layer on a parchment-lined air-fryer basket. Cook until edges are light brown, 8-12 minutes. Cool in basket 2 minutes. Remove to wire racks to cool completely.

4. In a small bowl, mix confectioners' sugar and enough lemon juice to reach a drizzling consistency. Drizzle over cookies. Let stand until set.

FREEZE OPTION: Place the wrapped rolls in a resealable container and freeze. To use, unwrap frozen rolls and cut into slices. Cook as directed, increasing time by 1-2 minutes. Prepare icing; drizzle as directed.

1 COOKIE: 110 cal., 4g fat (2g sat. fat), 18mg chol., 99mg sod., 17g carb. (11g sugars, 0 fiber), 1g pro.

Slice & Bake Fruitcake Cookies

A cross between classic fruitcake and buttery cookies, these treats are perfect for Christmas. Each one is chock-full of raisins and candied cherries.
—*Marlene Robinson, Sexsmith, AB*

PREP: 20 MIN. + CHILLING • **BAKE:** 15 MIN./BATCH • **MAKES:** 5 DOZEN

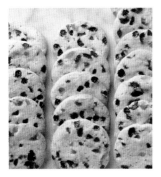

1. In a large bowl, cream butter and sugars until light and fluffy, 5-7 minutes. Beat in egg and vanilla. Combine flour and baking soda; gradually add to creamed mixture and mix well. Fold in raisins and cherries.

2. Shape dough into two 2-in.-diameter rolls; securely wrap each in waxed paper. Refrigerate for 2 hours or until firm.

3. Cut rolls into ¼-in. slices. Place 2 in. apart on ungreased baking sheets. Bake at 350° 12-15 minutes or until lightly browned. Remove to wire racks to cool.

1 cup butter, softened
1 cup confectioners' sugar
½ cup sugar
1 large egg, room temperature
2 tsp. vanilla extract
2¼ cups all-purpose flour
½ tsp. baking soda
½ cup raisins
½ cup each red and green candied cherries, chopped

1 COOKIE: 72 cal., 3g fat (2g sat. fat), 11mg chol., 38mg sod., 10g carb. (6g sugars, 0 fiber), 1g pro.

READER REVIEW
"I made these last year for the holidays. They topped my list of goodies to sneak when no one was looking! Absolutely delicious."
—CHARLENESMITH, TASTEOFHOME.COM

CHAPTER 7
No-Bake Cookies

Peppermint Candy Sandwich Cookies

I love to include a little homemade treat in teacher and hostess gifts, and these delicious lovelies (which come together in minutes) never fail to charm. They store well in an airtight container at room temperature.
—*Jennifer Beckman, Falls Church, VA*

TAKES: 20 MIN. • MAKES: 20 SANDWICH COOKIES

¼ cup butter, softened
¼ cup shortening
1 tsp. vanilla extract
½ tsp. peppermint extract
2 cups confectioners' sugar
½ cup finely crushed peppermint candies
1 pkg. (9 oz.) chocolate wafers

1. In a large bowl, beat butter, shortening and extracts until blended. Gradually beat in confectioners' sugar until thick and creamy. Stir in candies.

2. Spread about 1 Tbsp. mixture on bottoms of half the cookies. Cover with remaining cookies.

1 SANDWICH COOKIE: 154 cal., 7g fat (3g sat. fat), 6mg chol., 93mg sod., 24g carb. (18g sugars, 0 fiber), 1g pro.

NOTES

Crunchy Apricot-Coconut Balls

My mom gave me this no-bake cookie recipe years ago when she had them on her Christmas buffet. I can't believe how simple they are to make.

—*Jane Whittaker, Pensacola, FL*

TAKES: 30 MIN. • MAKES: 2 DOZEN

1¼ cups sweetened shredded coconut
1 cup dried apricots, finely chopped
⅔ cup chopped pecans
½ cup fat-free sweetened condensed milk
½ cup confectioners' sugar

1. In a small bowl, combine coconut, apricots and pecans. Add condensed milk; mix well (mixture will be sticky).

2. Shape into 1¼-in. balls and roll in confectioners' sugar. Store in an airtight container in the refrigerator.

1 BALL: 87 cal., 4g fat (2g sat. fat), 1mg chol., 19mg sod., 12g carb. (10g sugars, 1g fiber), 1g pro.

No-Bake Butterscotch Cookies

More like a candy than a cookie, these little butterscotch treats are delightful.
For a change, substitute chocolate fudge flavor pudding mix for the
butterscotch and use semisweet chocolate chips.
—*Andrea Price, Grafton, WI*

PREP: 20 MIN. + STANDING • **MAKES:** ABOUT 3 DOZEN

1. In a large saucepan, combine sugar, cubed butter and evaporated milk. Bring to a boil; boil for 1 minute. Remove from heat. Stir in pudding mix and oats until blended. Stir in chips and pecans.

2. Drop by tablespoonfuls 1 in. apart onto parchment-lined baking sheets. Let stand until set.

1 COOKIE: 150 cal., 7g fat (4g sat. fat), 11mg chol., 77mg sod., 21g carb. (16g sugars, 1g fiber), 2g pro.

2 cups sugar
¾ cup butter, cubed
1 can (5 oz.) evaporated milk
1 pkg. (3.4 oz.) instant butterscotch pudding mix
3½ cups old-fashioned oats
¾ cup butterscotch chips
½ cup chopped pecans

OATY OPTIONS
If you bought the wrong oats, it's not necessarily a disaster. Quick-cooking oats are just old-fashioned (aka rolled) oats that have been cut into smaller pieces so they'll cook faster. You can use quick oats, but there will be a difference in the texture of the finished cookies. If you bought steel-cut oats, however, it's best to make a return trip to the store. Steel-cut oats haven't been rolled, and are intended for long cooking; the result will be a tough, unpleasantly chewy cookie.

Buttery Lemon Sandwich Cookies

My grandson approves of these lemony sandwich cookies made with crackers and prepared frosting. Decorate with whatever sprinkles you'd like.
—*Nancy Foust, Stoneboro, PA*

PREP: 20 MIN. + STANDING • MAKES: 2½ DOZEN

1. Spread frosting on bottoms of half of the crackers; cover with the remaining crackers.

2. Dip sandwiches in melted candy coating; allow excess to drip off. Place on waxed paper; decorate as desired. Let stand until set. Store in an airtight container in the refrigerator.

1 SANDWICH COOKIE: 171 cal., 9g fat (6g sat. fat), 0 chol., 70mg sod., 23g carb. (19g sugars, 0 fiber), 0 pro.

¾ cup lemon frosting
60 Ritz crackers
24 oz. white candy coating, melted
    Optional: Nonpareils, jimmies or sprinkles

Black Forest Icebox Cookies

These rich chocolate wafers are the perfect complement to the
creamy filling's sweet-tart tones. Chill for up to four hours;
any longer and the wafers get too soft to pick up with your hands.
—Taste of Home *Test Kitchen*

PREP: 15 MIN. + CHILLING • **COOK:** 5 MIN. + COOLING • **MAKES:** 20 COOKIES

1. In a small saucepan, combine the sugar, cornstarch and salt. Add the cherries, juice blend and lemon juice. Bring to a boil; cook and stir until thickened, about 2 minutes. Remove from the heat; if desired, stir in food coloring. Cool to room temperature.

2. In a small bowl, combine the mascarpone cheese, confectioners' sugar and brandy. Spread about 1 tsp. cheese mixture onto each of 20 wafers; layer each with 2 tsp. cherry mixture. Top with remaining wafers. Place on a waxed paper-lined baking pan.

3   **Tbsp. sugar**
4   **tsp. cornstarch**
    Dash salt
¾   **cup fresh or frozen**
    pitted tart cherries
    (thawed), coarsely
    chopped
¾   **cup cherry juice blend**
1½ **tsp. lemon juice**
1   **to 2 drops red food**
    coloring, optional
½   **cup mascarpone**
    cheese
1   **Tbsp. confectioners'**
    sugar
1   **tsp. cherry brandy**
1   **pkg. (9 oz.) chocolate**
    wafers
½   **cup semisweet**
    chocolate chips
¼   **cup heavy whipping**
    cream

3. Place chocolate chips in a small bowl. In a small saucepan, bring cream just to a boil. Pour over chips; whisk until smooth. Drizzle over cookies. Refrigerate, covered, for up to 4 hours before serving.

1 SANDWICH COOKIE: 139 cal., 9g fat (4g sat. fat), 17mg chol., 81mg sod., 15g carb. (9g sugars, 1g fiber), 2g pro.

Christmas Mice Cookies

Add some whimsy to a cookie tray with these little cuties that taste like truffles. Every Christmas, we make sure to have enough for friends and neighbors.
—*Deborah Zabor, Fort Erie, ON*

PREP: 30 MIN. + CHILLING • MAKES: 1½ DOZEN

⅔ **cup semisweet chocolate chips**
2 **cups chocolate wafer crumbs, divided**
⅓ **cup sour cream**
36 **nonpareils**
¼ **cup sliced almonds**
18 **pieces black shoestring licorice (2 in. each)**

1. In a microwave, melt the chocolate chips; stir until smooth. Stir in 1 cup wafer crumbs and the sour cream. Refrigerate, covered, 1 hour or until firm enough to shape.

2. Place the remaining 1 cup wafer crumbs in a shallow bowl. For each mouse, roll about 1 Tbsp. chilled chocolate mixture into a ball; taper 1 end to resemble a mouse. Roll in wafer crumbs to coat. Attach nonpareils for eyes, sliced almonds for ears and licorice pieces for tails. Store in an airtight container in the refrigerator.

1 COOKIE: 135 cal., 5g fat (2g sat. fat), 3mg chol., 89mg sod., 22g carb. (11g sugars, 1g fiber), 2g pro. **DIABETIC EXCHANGES:** 1½ starch, ½ fat.

READER REVIEW
"I made these for a Christmas party—they were not only cute but also very tasty. I used chocolate graham crackers, then I made a batch using regular graham crackers. What a hoot!"
—GARALDINELOISMIDDLETON, TASTEOFHOME.COM

15-Minute Cookies

My mom used to pack these cookies into our school lunches.
They're inexpensive and easy to prepare, so all seven of us children
learned to make them. Now they're also a favorite with my two children.
—*Kerry Bouchard, Augusta, MT*

TAKES: 15 MIN. • MAKES: ABOUT 3 DOZEN

½ cup butter, cubed
½ cups 2% milk
2 cups sugar
3 cups quick-cooking
  oats or old-fashioned
  oats
5 Tbsp. baking cocoa
½ cup raisins, chopped
  nuts or sweetened
  shredded coconut

1. In a large saucepan, heat butter, milk and sugar. Bring to a boil, stirring occasionally. Boil for 1 minute.

2. Remove from the heat. Stir in the oats, cocoa, and raisins, nuts or coconut. Drop by tablespoonfuls onto waxed paper. Cool.

1 COOKIE: 101 cal., 3g fat (2g sat. fat), 7mg chol., 22mg sod., 18g carb. (13g sugars, 1g fiber), 1g pro.

Cannoli Wafer Sandwiches

My family loves to visit a local Italian restaurant that has a wonderful dessert buffet. The cannoli is among our favorite choices, so I just had to come up with my own simple version. These sandwiches are best when served the same day so the wafers remain nice and crisp.

—*Nichi Larson, Shawnee, KS*

PREP: 35 MIN. + STANDING •**MAKES:** 3½ DOZEN

1. In a small bowl, mix ricotta cheese, confectioners' sugar, sugar and vanilla until blended. Spread 1 scant tsp. filling on bottoms of half the wafers; cover with remaining wafers.

2. Dip each sandwich cookie halfway into the candy coating; allow the excess to drip off. Place on waxed paper; sprinkle with the chocolate chips. Let stand until set, about 10 minutes.

3. Serve within 2 hours or refrigerate until serving. Dust with additional confectioners' sugar just before serving.

1   **cup whole-milk ricotta cheese**
¼   **cup confectioners' sugar**
1   **Tbsp. sugar**
¼   **tsp. vanilla extract**
1   **pkg. (11 oz.) vanilla wafers**
12 **oz. white candy coating, melted**
½   **cup miniature semisweet chocolate chips**
    Additional confectioners' sugar

1 SANDWICH COOKIE: 93 cal., 5g fat (3g sat. fat), 4mg chol., 38mg sod., 13g carb. (10g sugars, 0 fiber), 1g pro.

Chocolate Butterscotch Haystacks

My grandmother made haystacks like these and slipped them to my cousin Vonnie and me when our parents didn't want us to have any more sweets.
—*Christine Schwester, Divide, CO*

PREP: 25 MIN. + CHILLING • **MAKES:** 3 DOZEN

1. In a microwave or on the stovetop in a large metal bowl over simmering water, melt chocolate chips and butterscotch chips; stir until smooth. Gently stir in noodles.

2. Drop by rounded tablespoonfuls onto waxed paper-lined baking sheets. Refrigerate 10-15 minutes or until set.

1 HAYSTACK: 160 cal., 9g fat (5g sat. fat), 0 chol., 84mg sod., 22g carb. (15g sugars, 1g fiber), 1g pro.

2 cups semisweet chocolate chips
1 pkg. (10 to 11 oz.) butterscotch chips
4 cups crispy chow mein noodles

STACK 'EM HOW YOU LIKE 'EM
It's easy to make these haystacks your own! It can be as simple as adding your favorite nuts or dried fruit, or you can even experiment with seasonal flavors of baking chips. There are lots on the market—including cinnamon, espresso, caramel, peppermint, peanut butter and Irish cream.

Frosty Polar Bears

I love spending time in the kitchen with my nieces. This is the perfect recipe to make with the little ones. Dang cute, easy and portable!
—*Emily Tyra, Lake Ann, MI*

PREP: 25 MIN. + CHILLING • MAKES: 2½ DOZEN

¾ **cup creamy peanut butter**
60 **Ritz crackers**
24 **oz. white candy coating, melted**
60 **miniature marshmallows**
30 **mini Ritz crackers**
Blue chocolate M&M's
Black sugar pearls
Black decorating icing, optional

1. Spread peanut butter on half of the crackers; top with remaining crackers to make sandwiches. Refrigerate until firm.

2. Dip sandwiches in melted candy coating; allow excess to drip off. Place on waxed paper. Dip marshmallows in coating; allow excess to drip off. Place 2 marshmallows on top of each cookie for ears.

3. Dip mini crackers in melted candy coating; allow excess to drip off. Place on top of sandwiches for snouts. Top each snout with a blue M&M. Decorate with black sugar pearls for eyes and, if desired, use black decorating icing for mouths. Let stand until set. Refrigerate cookies in an airtight container.

1 SANDWICH COOKIE: 201 cal., 12g fat (7g sat. fat), 0 chol., 112mg sod., 23g carb. (16g sugars, 0 fiber), 2g pro.

MIX UP THE FLAVORS
Nutella and cookie butter are delicious substitutes for peanut butter. When the holiday season is over, take these bears from the North Pole to the North Woods by dipping them in milk or dark chocolate candy coating.

Chocolate Caramel Wafers

To keep my holiday cooking quick, I've come to rely on fast recipes like this one. The crunchy-chewy tidbits are our youngster's favorite.
—*Susan Laubach, Vida, MT*

TAKES: 30 MIN. • **MAKES:** 7 DOZEN

1. Place caramels and milk in a microwave-safe bowl; microwave, uncovered, on high for 2 minutes or until caramels are melted. Stir until smooth. Spread over vanilla wafers; place on ungreased baking sheets.

2. Top each with a chocolate square. Place in a 225° oven for 1-2 minutes or until chocolate is melted. Spread with an icing knife. Sprinkle with pecans if desired.

1 COOKIE: 60 cal., 2g fat (1g sat. fat), 2mg chol., 31mg sod., 9g carb. (7g sugars, 0 fiber), 1g pro.

1 pkg. (14 oz.) caramels
¼ cup evaporated milk
1 pkg. (12 oz.) vanilla wafers
8 plain milk chocolate candy bars (1.55 oz. each), broken into squares
   Chopped pecans, optional

No-Bake Peanut Brownies

You can enlist the kids to help make these chocolaty peanut butter brownies.
I like the fact that I can enjoy them but keep my oven free.
—*Connie Ward, Mount Pleasant, IA*

PREP: 25 MIN. + CHILLING • MAKES: 16 SERVINGS

4   cups graham cracker crumbs
1   cup chopped peanuts
½   cup confectioners' sugar
¼   cup peanut butter
2   cups semisweet chocolate chips
¾   cup evaporated milk
1   tsp. vanilla extract

1. In a large bowl, combine the crumbs, peanuts, confectioners' sugar and peanut butter until crumbly. In a small saucepan, melt the chocolate chips and milk over low heat, stirring constantly until smooth. Remove from the heat; add vanilla.

2. Pour the chocolate mixture over the crumb mixture and stir until well blended. Spread evenly in a greased 9-in. square dish. Cover and refrigerate for 1 hour.

1 BROWNIE: 169 cal., 9g fat (3g sat. fat), 2mg chol., 78mg sod., 22g carb. (12g sugars, 2g fiber), 3g pro.

NOTES

Gooey Caramel-Topped Gingersnaps

Making these cookies is therapeutic for me. These gingersnaps are quite popular at fundraisers. If you'd like, you can make variations by changing the cookie base or varying the nuts.
—*Deirdre Cox, Kansas City, MO*

PREP: 30 MIN. + CHILLING • **MAKES:** 3½ DOZEN

1. Arrange cookies in a single layer on waxed paper-lined baking sheets. In a microwave, melt caramels with milk; stir until smooth. Stir in 1 cup chopped peanuts. Spoon about 1 tsp. caramel mixture over each cookie; refrigerate until set.

2. Dip each cookie halfway into candy coating; allow excess to drip off. Return to baking sheet; top with sprinkles or finely chopped peanuts. Refrigerate until set.

1 COOKIE: 128 cal., 5g fat (3g sat. fat), 1mg chol., 70mg sod., 19g carb. (14g sugars, 0 fiber), 2g pro.

42 **gingersnap cookies**
1 **pkg. (14 oz.) caramels**
2 **Tbsp. 2% milk or heavy whipping cream**
1 **cup chopped honey-roasted peanuts**
12 **oz. white or dark chocolate candy coating, melted**
Sprinkles or finely chopped honey-roasted peanuts

Peanut Butter Pretzel Bars

My secret to these rich no-bake bites? Pretzels in the crust.
They add a salty crunch to the classic peanut butter and chocolate pairing.
—*Jennifer Beckman, Falls Church, VA*

PREP: 15 MIN. + CHILLING • **MAKES:** 4 DOZEN

1 **pkg. (16 oz.) miniature pretzels, divided**
1½ **cups butter, melted**
1½ **cups peanut butter**
3 **cups confectioners' sugar**
2 **cups semisweet chocolate chips**
1 **Tbsp. shortening**

1. Line a 13x9-in. baking pan with foil, letting ends extend up sides. Set aside 1½ cups pretzels for topping. In a food processor, pulse the remaining pretzels until fine crumbs form. In a large bowl, mix the melted butter, peanut butter, confectioners' sugar and pretzel crumbs.

2. Press mixture into prepared pan. In a microwave, melt chocolate chips and shortening; stir until smooth. Spread over peanut butter layer. Break reserved pretzels and sprinkle over top; press down gently. Refrigerate, covered, until set, about 1 hour. Lifting with foil, remove from pan. Cut into bars.

1 BAR: 201 cal., 13g fat (6g sat. fat), 15mg chol., 233mg sod., 22g carb. (12g sugars, 1g fiber), 3g pro.

WHAT'S THE BUTTER CHOICE?
Unless otherwise specified, *Taste of Home* recipes are tested with lightly salted butter. Unsalted, or sweet, butter is sometimes used when added salt would detract from the buttery taste desired, as in shortbread cookies or buttercream frosting.

Nutty Rice Krispie Cookies

My mom and I used to prepare these treats for Christmas every year. Making them with just the microwave means they're super easy and fun to mix with the kids.
—*Savanna Chapdelaine, Orlando, FL*

PREP: 15 MIN. + COOLING • **MAKES:** ABOUT 2 DOZEN

1. In a large microwave-safe bowl, melt baking chips; stir until smooth. Stir in peanut butter until blended. Add marshmallows, Rice Krispies and peanuts.

2. Drop mixture by heaping tablespoonfuls onto waxed paper-lined baking sheets. Cool completely. Store in an airtight container.

1 COOKIE: 127 cal., 8g fat (3g sat. fat), 2mg chol., 49mg sod., 11g carb. (9g sugars, 1g fiber), 3g pro.

1   pkg. (10 to 12 oz.) white baking chips
¼   cup creamy peanut butter
1   cup miniature marshmallows
1   cup Rice Krispies
1   cup salted peanuts

A KRISPIE BY ANY OTHER NAME...
Despite their name, these cookies can be made with cereals other than Rice Krispies! Using cereal as an ingredient in recipes can give you lots of distinctive flavors and textures. Try using cornflakes, Cinnamon Toast Crunch, or any kind of Chex cereal.

It's not just the cereal, either—this is one of the best cookie recipes when it comes to customizing your ingredients. Don't like peanuts? Swap in other nuts, such as walnuts, pistachios or cashews. You can even use candies instead, like M&M's. Not a fan of white chocolate? Substitute regular chocolate chips instead. Get creative!

Yummy Cracker Snacks

These treats are my family's favorite, and it seems no matter how many I make, they always disappear too soon.
—*D. Weaver, Ephrata, PA*

PREP: 1 HOUR + CHILLING • **MAKES:** 4 DOZEN

1. Spread half of the crackers with peanut butter. Spread remaining crackers with marshmallow creme; place creme side down over peanut butter crackers, forming a sandwich. Place on waxed paper-lined pans; freeze for 15 minutes or until firm.

2. Dip sandwiches in melted candy coating, allowing excess to drip off. If desired, drizzle with additional candy coating and decorate with sprinkles. Store in an airtight container.

1 CRACKER SNACK: 170 cal., 10g fat (6g sat. fat), 0 chol., 89mg sod., 19g carb. (14g sugars, 1g fiber), 2g pro.

96 Ritz crackers
 1 cup creamy peanut butter
 1 cup marshmallow creme
 2 lbs. milk chocolate candy coating, melted
   Sprinkles, optional

Easy Peanut Butter Balls

These simple saucepan cookies are a snap to make. In fact, I can whip them up in minutes for school lunches. The little treats are a big hit with any crowd—young or old.
—*Marg Mitro, Grafton, ON*

TAKES: 20 MIN. • MAKES: 4 DOZEN

1 cup **light corn syrup**
½ cup **sugar**
1 cup **peanut butter**
1 tsp. **vanilla extract**
4 to 5 cups **cornflakes**

1. In a large saucepan, bring the corn syrup and sugar to a boil. Add the peanut butter. Remove from the heat; stir in vanilla and cornflakes.

2. Drop by tablespoonfuls onto waxed paper. Store in an airtight container.

1 PEANUT BUTTER BALL: 69 cal., 3g fat (1g sat. fat), 0 chol., 44mg sod., 11g carb. (9g sugars, 0 fiber), 1g pro.

A COUPLE OF QUICK NO-NOS
Do not use natural or low-fat peanut butter for this recipe—the consistency is different and your peanut butter balls might not set properly.

Also, it's best to make and eat these treats fresh (stored correctly, they'll last about 3 days at room temperature), as opposed to freezing them. If you freeze them, they may become soggy.

Chocolate Rum Balls

Roll these truffle-like rum balls in crushed Oreos to get just the right amount of crunch. I've been known to freeze them for emergencies.
—*Dauna Harwood, Elkhart, IN*

PREP: 30 MIN. + CHILLING • **MAKES:** ABOUT 3 DOZEN

1. Dissolve coffee granules in warm rum. Beat cream cheese, confectioners' sugar, almonds and rum mixture until blended. Stir in melted chocolate. Refrigerate until firm enough to roll, about 1 hour.

2. Shape mixture into 1-in. balls; roll in crushed cookies. Store in an airtight container in the refrigerator, separating layers with waxed paper.

1 RUM BALL: 70 cal., 4g fat (2g sat. fat), 3mg chol., 21mg sod., 7g carb. (5g sugars, 1g fiber), 1g pro.

1 tsp. instant coffee granules
¼ cup dark rum, warmed
4 oz. cream cheese, softened
1 cup confectioners' sugar
1 cup ground almonds
3 oz. unsweetened chocolate, melted
8 Oreo cookies, finely crushed

READER REVIEW

"Fantastic! I was looking for a variation to the chocolate rum balls I usually make. I came across this recipe that is not the typical no-bake, super-sweet version. The cream cheese offsets the sugar for a perfect balance. I normally roll mine in walnuts but love the Oreo crumbs!"
—SUEFALK, TASTEOFHOME.COM

Easy Mint Thins

*My friends often try to guess the ingredients in these cookies,
but I never tell them how simple they are to make.*
—*Jennifer Setser, Morgantown, IN*

PREP: 40 MIN. + STANDING • **MAKES:** 5 DOZEN

1. In a microwave, melt chocolate candy coating; stir until smooth. Stir in extract.

2. Dip crackers in chocolate candy coating; allow excess to drip off. Place on waxed paper; let stand until set.

3. Drizzle tops with white candy coating; decorate as desired. Let stand until set. Store in airtight containers.

1 COOKIE: 89 cal., 4g fat (2g sat. fat), 0 chol., 34mg sod., 9g carb. (6g sugars, 0 fiber), 1g pro.

24 oz. milk or dark
  chocolate candy
  coating
1½ tsp. peppermint extract
60 Ritz crackers
2 oz. white candy coating,
  melted
  Optional decorations:
  Chopped Andes mint
  candies, crushed
  spearmint candies,
  assorted sprinkles and
  green colored sugar

Cherry No-Bake Cookies

I always loved my no-bake cookie recipe, but I was never able to place at the fair with it. So I mixed in some maraschino cherries, added almond extract, and voila! I won a blue ribbon at the county fair.
—*Denise Wheeler, Newaygo, MI*

PREP: 30 MIN. + CHILLING • **MAKES:** ABOUT 5½ DOZEN

1. In a large saucepan, combine sugar, butter, milk and cocoa. Bring to a boil, stirring constantly. Cook and stir for 3 minutes.

2. Remove from heat; stir in peanut butter and extracts until blended. Stir in oats and cherries.

3. Drop mixture by tablespoonfuls onto waxed paper-lined baking sheets. Refrigerate until set. Store in airtight containers.

1 COOKIE: 81 cal., 4g fat (1g sat. fat), 4mg chol., 29mg sod., 11g carb. (8g sugars, 1g fiber), 2g pro.

2 cups sugar
½ cup butter, cubed
6 Tbsp. 2% milk
3 Tbsp. baking cocoa
1 cup peanut butter
½ tsp. vanilla extract
¼ tsp. almond extract
3 cups quick-cooking oats
1 jar (10 oz.) maraschino cherries, well drained and finely chopped

Chocolate Lebkuchen Cherry Balls

Here's my twist on the traditional German holiday lebkuchen—with a surprise inside.
Maraschino cherries add a sweet and unexpected punch to the holiday spice of gingersnaps.
—Arlene Erlbach, Morton Grove, IL

PREP: 45 MIN. + CHILLING • MAKES: 5 DOZEN

40 gingersnap cookies
1 pkg. (8 oz.) cream
cheese, softened
1½ cups semisweet
chocolate chips, divided
1¼ cups sliced almonds,
divided
2 Tbsp. chopped candied
orange peel
1 tsp. almond extract
60 maraschino cherries,
stems removed

1. Place gingersnaps, cream cheese, ½ cup chocolate chips, ½ cup almonds, the orange peel and extract in a food processor; process until combined. Refrigerate until firm enough to form into balls.

2. Pat cherries dry with paper towels. Wrap each cherry with a rounded tablespoon cream cheese mixture; shape into a ball. Freeze until balls are firm, about 20 minutes.

3. Chop remaining ¾ cup sliced almonds; set aside. In a double boiler, melt remaining 1 cup chocolate chips; stir until smooth. Dip cherry balls in chocolate; allow excess to drip off. Sprinkle balls with almonds. Place on waxed paper. Refrigerate until set, about 1 hour.

1 BALL: 76 cal., 4g fat (2g sat. fat), 4mg chol., 37mg sod., 10g carb. (7g sugars, 1g fiber), 1g pro.

Holiday Reindeer Cookies

Set these cute no-bake cookies out for Santa on Christmas Eve.
If you listen closely, you might hear reindeer hooves on the roof!
—Taste of Home *Test Kitchen*

PREP: 45 MIN. + STANDING • MAKES: 32 COOKIES

1½ **lbs. dark chocolate
candy coating, chopped**
1 **pkg. (16 oz.) Nutter
Butter cookies**
32 **miniature
marshmallows,
cut in half crosswise
Decorating icing**
32 **M&M's or Red Hots**
64 **miniature pretzels**

1. In a microwave, melt candy coating; stir until smooth. Dip 1 cookie in chocolate; allow excess to drip off. Place on waxed paper.

2. Attach 2 marshmallow halves onto cookie for eyes; add decorating icing for pupils and a mouth. Add an M&M or Red Hot for nose. Attach pretzels or pretzel pieces for antlers. Repeat with remaining cookies. Let stand until set.

1 COOKIE: 182 cal., 9g fat (4g sat. fat), 0 chol., 111mg sod., 24g carb. (16g sugars, 0 fiber), 3g pro.

Recipe Index

1, 2, 3

A

B

C

D